WHEN LIFE IS
HARD

James
MacDonald

MOODY PUBLISHERS
CHICAGO

All Scripture quotations, unless otherwise indicated, are taken from *The Holy Bible, English Standard Version.* Copyright © 2000, 2001 by Crossway Bibles, a division of Good News Publishers. Used by permission. All rights reserved.

Scripture quotations marked NKJV are taken from the *New King James Version.* Copyright © 1982 by Thomas Nelson, Inc. Used by permission. All rights reserved.

Scripture quotations marked NASB are taken from the *New American Standard Bible®*, Copyright © 1960, 1962, 1963, 1968, 1971, 1972, 1973, 1975, 1977, 1995 by The Lockman Foundation. Used by permission. (www.Lockman.org)

Published in association with the literary agency of Wolgemuth & Associates, Inc.

Editor: Jim Vincent
Interior Design: Smartt Guys design
Cover Design: David Riley Associates
Cover Image: i-stock, 2874282, misty-morning-tree

Library of Congress Cataloging-in-Publication Data

MacDonald, James, 1960-
　When life is hard / James MacDonald.
　　p. cm.
　Includes bibliographical references.
　ISBN 978-0-8024-5871-1
　　1. Consolation. 2. Providence and government of God—Christianity. 3. Trust in God—Christianity. I. Title.
BV4905.3.M29 2010
248.8'6—dc22

2009042926

We hope you enjoy this book from Moody Publishers. Our goal is to provide high-quality, thought-provoking books and products that connect truth to your real needs and chal-lenges. For more information on other books and products written and produced from a biblical perspective, go to www.moodypublishers.com or write to:

Moody Publishers
820 N. LaSalle Boulevard
Chicago, IL 60610

1 3 5 7 9 10 8 6 4 2

Printed in the United States of America

To my mom, Lorna MacDonald,
an exemplary follower of Jesus, and
only more so in the furnace of adversity!

He knows the way that I take;
when he has tried me, I shall come out as gold.
Job 23:10

CONTENTS

Foreword   7

Introduction: In the Middle of a Category 5 Hurricane   9

How to Get the Most from This Book   15

1. What Are Trials?   23

2. Why Trials?   47

3. What to Do with Trials   75

4. What If I Refuse This Trial?   99

5. Why Some Trials Never End   123

6. Come Forth as Gold   149

     PRINCIPLE 1: Every trial I face is allowed by God for my ultimate good.   153

     PRINCIPLE 2: Trials need not steal my joy.   163

     PRINCIPLE 3: God is never more present than when His children are suffering.   173

     PRINCIPLE 4: Until I embrace my trial in unwavering submission to God, I will not reap the good.   183

Epilogue: This Trial Could Be the Best Thing That's Ever Happened to You   197

Notes   201

Acknowledgments   203

GLIMPSES OF GOLD

GLIMPSE OF GOLD 1: *God knows.*   21

GLIMPSE OF GOLD 2: *God sees.*   45

GLIMPSE OF GOLD 3: *God measures.*   73

GLIMPSE OF GOLD 4: *God initiates.*   97

GLIMPSE OF GOLD 5: *God reveals.*   121

GLIMPSE OF GOLD 6: *God refines.*   147

FOREWORD

A poll by the Barna Group once asked, "If you could ask God one question, and you knew that He would give you an answer, what would you ask?" The most common response was, "Why is there pain and suffering in the world?"

If you share the gospel with someone who does not yet know the Lord, it won't be long before they ask, "How could a God of love allow tragedy, pain, and suffering?" In fact, C. S. Lewis said that "the problem of pain is atheism's most potent weapon against the Christian faith."

Perhaps you, or someone you know, have recently faced tragedy or received some really bad news and you are wondering, "Why?" When a tsunami or earthquake hits and thousands die, we wonder, "Why?" A child is born with a disability and we wonder, "Why?" A Christian friend gets cancer and we wonder, "Why?"

A young man is killed in an automobile accident and we wonder,

"Why?" Our family had to face this very tragedy with the early departure to heaven of our oldest son, Christopher, in 2008.

Even Christians ask, "Why?" That is why I am so glad that my good friend James MacDonald has tackled this vital and gnawing subject in his new book *When Life Is Hard.*

Know this—James is not offering pious platitudes from an ivory tower of mere theory. Rather, he is writing from the place of pain, as James himself was recently diagnosed with cancer in 2008. Thankfully, his treatments have been successful, but James has certainly suffered and is qualified to speak on this topic, not only as a powerful teacher of God's Word but also as a fellow traveler on the road of pain.

While he was getting medical attention for his cancer in Southern California, James asked if he could preach a series of sermons at our church that could be taped and shown to his home congregation at Harvest Bible Chapel in Chicago. Of course, I agreed. As I listened to these messages, which were very well received, I told him, "You must put these in a book!" And you are now holding this result.

I am delighted to now encourage you to read what James has learned from both Scripture and life on the topic of pain and suffering, and find much needed hope.

GREG LAURIE
Senior Pastor, Harvest Christian Fellowship
Riverside, California

In the Middle of
a Category 5
HURRICANE

In the midst of the storm it's difficult to know when you heard the first thunderclap. For me, it was sometime during the summer of 2004.

Our church was growing rapidly toward and beyond the 10,000 attendance mark and we had undertaken a very ambitious ministry/facility expansion. More than twenty million dollars had been pledged, and we planned to spend almost double that amount building a camp and starting a new K-12 Christian school. We had also begun erecting a 300,000 square foot worship complex on our newest campus.

During this time our radio ministry, "Walk in the Word," was growing into an exciting partnership with a popular out-of-state ministry, bringing explosive growth and impact. I was writing books, launching a revival ministry attended by thousands in arenas around the country, and my wife and I were enjoying our three teenage children.

Looking back, I should have checked into a mental hospital for allowing all that to go on at once. It's not like people didn't try to warn me, it's just that I knew God was bigger than all the challenges and I was blindly in-tent on "seizing the opportunity."

I'm not sure when we heard the first rumble of thunder, but sometime during the summer of 2004 my wife and I sailed into a gale that became over three years a storm and finally a category 5 hurricane. "Landfall" for the hurricane would come in late 2007.

Our oldest son broke his neck in a serious car accident and came within a hair's width of death. For several months we would take Luke back and forth to doctors in his skull-piercing metal "halo," continuing to pray that his blood supply would get to the remote area in his neck. For most people, such a condition seldom heals without surgery—surgery in the vocal re-gion that would imperil his gift of leading worship.

At the same time, a wonderful treasure of a young man in our church was gone from this earth in a moment. The news of Mitch's tragic drown-ing came to his parents when my wife and I were with them. They are among our closest friends, and our shared grief was beyond description. I will neither forget that night nor the days, weeks, and months that followed such an earth-shattering loss.

Soon, one of the founding elders of our church died and two other eld-ers faced cancer in their families, one with a son, another with his wife.

Due to circumstances outside my direct control, our construction budget was over by $20 million, staff had to be fired, and I was dragged into the middle of it all. Then irregularities in the structural steel halted work for seven months, requiring a multimillion dollar fix that was hard to config-ure and almost impossible to fund.

Millions of dollars of liens were placed on the stalled project, and dark clouds of bankruptcy loomed large over the entire ministry. Construction committee members resigned *en masse*. Night after night I walked alone through the incomplete worship facility. It felt more like a tomb than a church. As I walked I wondered how it had all come to this and what God's possible purpose could be in making life so hard.

Then our radio ministry partnership began to struggle and finally dissolve in the disillusionment of failed relationships and broken promises. But soon a replacement partnership from another solid ministry appeared. Painfully, after several hopeful months, this also perished in a way that made the first breakup seem inconsequential and leaving the international teaching ministry we had built over ten years also teetering on the edge of financial ruin.

The revival ministry called "Downpour" blessed thousands through our partnership with such gifted teachers as Beth Moore and Crawford Loritts, but then it faded as fast as it had flourished as demands on the church-front made travel impossible for me. During this season several of our key staff leaders left for a variety of good and not so good reasons; I could hardly blame them, as I was also casting about wondering if God would give me an exit ramp from this onslaught. Just as one trial, such as getting our church building done, would end, we would launch into another such as the national economy collapsing.

The hurricane had blown ashore, and everywhere we saw the storm's onslaught. The term *shell-shocked* would have been an understatement.

During this same season family issues at home took my understanding of despair to a level I could never have conceived. I learned the meaning of lying on my face and pooling my tears as I cried out to God. David's plea became very real to me: **"My tears have been my food day and night, while they say to me all the day long, 'Where is your God?'"** (Psalm 42:3).

Does that sound like enough trials? I certainly thought so as I pored over the Psalms and joined their pleading prayers for relief. Apparently God wanted us to experience a category 5 hurricane, because by the fall of 2008 I discovered that my lifetime of continual physical health had been eclipsed by prostate cancer.

That news rocked me to the core. Then came the devastating news my mother, the greatest source of prayer and blessing for Kathy and me, was diagnosed with a terminal disease that silenced her voice and slowed her pace to a near standstill. Now the hurricane smashed inland. Yes, life was hard. Very hard!

Where do you go at a time like this? How can you make sense from such a cascade of calamity? I hope you never have to find out; but I *did* have to.

Over Thanksgiving I researched my treatment options and chose a regimen of proton radiation therapy at Loma Linda University Medical Center in California. People kept asking about my cancer, but to be frank, my biggest burdens by far, were not physical. I needed some help and I needed it fast. I began to search the New Testament for what God had to say about trials. Not as an academic or a person called to feed the faith of others, but as a desperate soul crying out for some rain to soften the soil, for some nourishment to fill my hungry heart, for something, anything, to help me find my way out of the wasteland I once called a life.

I distanced myself from everyone, afraid of the pain of explaining how I was doing. Friends were leaving me alone—it was just me and God with my Bible open and a faithful praying wife standing, as always, by my side.

Loma Linda is 1,986 miles away from our kids and church family and the treatment required eleven weeks. Our church leaders were surprised I agreed to fill the pulpit of my dear friend Greg Laurie, pastor of Harvest Christian Fellowship in Riverside, California. I agreed to give six messages while in California, not because I couldn't be away from preaching, not because I could use the content in my own church by video, but because I was fearful of the impact of delaying my desperate need for biblical answers. Greg was enduring his own crucible in the sudden death of his firstborn son, and for that reason we were both very thirsty to learn what God has to say about crushing times in the lives of His children.

It was not the cancer treatment alone that made this time so difficult but the culmination of all that we had been seeking to endure. Every day for ten weeks it was pretty much the same schedule: cancer treatments in the morning and then deeply into God's Word in the afternoons to feed my own weary soul. Then weekly I would get up and preach what I was learning about what I was going through. Afterward I would try to rest for a day and then start the cycle again.

You can be sure that nothing shallow or superficial got into those messages. They were preached during a time of economic collapse and a transition to a new American president. I knew that people's hearts were hurting and hungering for nourishing insights for their own famished faith. The messages did end up being shown by video to our own church almost simultaneously. For that reason I felt the pressure of almost 25,000 people between our two churches looking for, even demanding answers for what they themselves were facing.

What God gave me during those weeks has changed my life, two churches, and countless other lives since that time. You now hold the written version in your hands. If life has been hard for you recently, maybe harder than you ever dreamed or thought possible, you are in the right place.

Week by week I was like the farmer in the field bringing the crops in and putting them on the table for supper that night. Everything delivered was fresh from the field. I was living it and still am to a great extent. And I'll be honest with you, some days are better than others. If you're in a trial right now, you know all about that, too.

When a hurricane blows into *your* life, you have to do more than hide behind boarded windows or flee to higher ground. My Scripture study uncovered powerful answers. When life is hard, we can learn much about who God is and how to access His strength. If you realize you cannot endure much longer—if you fear the strong gusts rattling your windows right now—I get it. And I can't wait to share with you what the Lord has revealed to me . . .

How to Get the
Most from This
BOOK

When you recognize there are six billion people in the world right now, all of them living their own lives, you begin to understand that what separates us is not *what* we're going through because into every life tribulation comes. The great divider is *how* we handle the times when life is hard.

I'll tell you how I'm handling it—I'm going after God. I believe it is in His good providence that we have connected this way.

So what's next? In this study, we'll be digging into key New Testament passages specifically dealing with how to go through hard times. By the end of it, we're going to know what God wants us to know when life is hard. And let's agree now that we are going to do what God wants us to *do* when life is hard. One of the things that has sustained me this past year is the hope that what I have been going through can be used by God to help others in a similar place. No one just casually picks up a book about trials. I am guessing you must be struggling under the weight of something. It may be a trial hard and huge that has invaded your life, something fearful that terrorizes your thoughts.

Or perhaps you have come through a recent struggle. You feel battered—maybe cynical or angry toward God. People don't read such books when life is firing on all cylinders, so I know by sheer deduction that your heart is heavy in some way and looking for help.

Can I say I'm sorry for your pain? Really I am. I'm praying even this moment that what you'll gain from these pages will bring you relief, wisdom, comfort—even joy as you walk through this season of adversity. Friend, if life is especially hard right now, my word for you is, Don't waste it! Don't go through these hard times and then, at the end, not even see the purpose for it or get the good God intended for you. Open your life wide to what God wants to accomplish in you.

As you read this book, you'll see some areas are not covered. **In fact, here's...**

WHAT YOU'RE *NOT* GOING TO FIND IN THIS BOOK:

Coping mechanisms. You're not going to get a list of *100 Ways to Be Happy in Your Trial.* Go online or to your favorite candy floss bookstore to find easy relief and then, be happy for two minutes before the next wave knocks you down even harder.

Existential musing. You're also not going to find answers to why there's pain in the universe. I believe God does provide us with answers that satisfy the human condition, but this is not a book about that.

Personal answers. You're also not going to get justifiable reasons for your specific personal pain: *Why did God allow me to get cancer . . . or my marriage to fail . . . or that car accident to happen . . . or my daughter to rebel . . . or my business to collapse?* However, you may get insight into what God wants to do in your life through it. In fact, before you begin, please read pages 197–200 in the back of the book called,

"This trial could be the best thing that's ever happened to you."

It may be hard to see them right now, but God does have some plans for you—plans for how to use this pain you're enduring. Jeremiah 29:11 says **"He knows the plans He has for you, plans to give you a future and a hope."**

Yes! That's what I want to hear, you may be thinking. *Let's get on those plans right now—future, hope, blessing. I'm ready!*

But here's the thing: God knows something else. He knows that we're not always ready for the plans that He has for us. So He has some plans to get us ready for His plans. That's really what this book is about—taking the difficult things that God allows into your life, and getting to the place where the blessing can be received.

To that goal, here's how to get the most from this study:

1. *Make it personal.* Don't read these pages with a sense of detached analytical evaluation. If you're into that, there are plenty of other books better for you. Only continue if you're ready to really enter in. WARNING: *There may be things here that are hard to read, but hard truths are the only way out of a hard place.* Promise yourself now that you are not going to explain away or excuse yourself from the things God wants to teach you. He wants pain to have its purpose in your life even more than you do. He wants to get you out and on to a better place but you control the schedule. Determine in your heart to approach this teaching with the attitude, *Whatever You want to show me, Lord, I'm listening.*

2. *Make it specific.* What is the painful circumstance allowed by God to refine your conduct and your character? Gather it up right now in your hand; you know what it is. Be specific with God and He will be specific with you. Before you begin each chapter—or each page or

each paragraph, ask yourself, *Will I submit to God in this? Am I commit-ted to working on myself and leaving God to work on what I cannot change? Will I trust God to handle this in His time and in His way? If not yet, am I willing to let God lead me to that place as I let His Word speak to me?*

3. *Give yourself to it.* Fully engage. Do the hard work of homework. This book is not a snooze in the warm sunshine; it is a road map to a better place that has some hill climbing involved.

We've provided several ways for you to download the truth into the center of your soul. Here are just a few:

- **GLIMPSES OF GOLD:** One of the metaphors that God uses to describe His purpose for trials is the process of refining gold. Job 23:10 is the most familiar and also the theme verse for this study. At the beginning of every chapter, we're going to mine the treasure from that verse, word by word. Don't rush past this gold mine. Take time to meditate upon this life-changing assurance from the Lord. It's a verse that has truly sustained me in some very dark times. I want it to mean to you what it has meant to me, so that's where we will start every chapter.

- **FROM GOD'S HEART TO MINE:** At the end of each chapter will be a couple of verses or a short Scripture passage that you just flat out need to have for yourself. Memorize it; take it personally. Nothing will be more comforting and sustaining to you than God's Word. Make it your own and you will benefit immensely and continually.

- **MINING FOR GOLD:** Each chapter includes a set of personal questions designed to help you reflect on and implement what God is showing you about trials in your life. This will allow you to apply the truth of God's Word to your personal situation.

• **COME FORTH AS GOLD:** The final chapter of this book has an unusual format. It includes a series of brief meditations on the key Bible passages related to personal trials. You can read through these brief lessons at a sitting, but you will want to return to them during times of trial. This chapter looks at the sixteen key lessons we've covered, and summarizes them in a get-it-and-run format. We've put each lesson on its own page so there's room at the end of each to write your own personal notes about how God is making this truth real in your life. Your notes may include dates and occasions when this particular truth for God's Word spoke into a hard time in your life.

In addition, you will find other tools at a special website, www.whenlifeishard.com. For those interested in having a small group discussion, chapter by chapter, a special discussion guide, "Sharing the Gold," awaits. "Like Mining the Gold" in this book, "Sharing" includes several questions per chapter that will help you review and apply biblical truths about trials, this time in a group setting where you can learn from one another.

As you go through this book and apply its lessons, remember and rest in this promise from the Word of God: "For the moment, all discipline seems painful rather than pleasant, but later it yields the peaceful fruit of righteousness to those who have been trained by it" (Hebrews 12:11).

But he knows *the way that I take;*

when he has tried me, I shall come out as gold. Job 23:10

God Knows

He sees me in this trial.

The fact that God knows you is the hinge pin that secures the truth of Scripture to your life. Truth and doctrine and everything God has revealed become personal because God declares that He knows you. He knows everything about you. He knows the way that you take. He knows your thoughts and ambitions. He knows your fears and motivations far more than you could conceive or imagine. He knows your address both now and in eternity.

That's an astounding fact. The Creator of the universe, the One who set the world in motion and who by the order of His hand keeps everything spinning—from the galaxies to every strand of your DNA—*this God* knows *you.*

He knows you better than you know yourself. God knows the number of hairs on your head (Matthew 10:30). God knows when you're crying, and puts your tears in a bottle (see Psalm 56:8). He's not missing a single detail of your life. He hears your conversations with your spouse. He sees your checkbook.

He knows your unspoken anxieties, even things you can't quite put your finger on. He's also watching the depth of your trial. He's monitoring the heat of the furnace. He's pouring out the strength that you need, to endure at the moment you feel you can't go on.

*And have you forgotten the exhortation that addresses you as sons?
"My son, do not regard lightly the discipline of the Lord, nor be weary
when reproved by him. For the Lord disciplines the one he loves, and chastises every son whom he receives." It is for discipline that you have to endure. God is treating you as sons. For what son is there whom his father
does not discipline? If you are left without discipline, in which all have
participated, then you are illegitimate children and not sons. Besides this,
we have had earthly fathers who disciplined us and we respected them.
Shall we not much more be subject to the Father of spirits and live? For
they disciplined us for a short time as it seemed best to them, but he disciplines us for our good, that we may share his holiness. For the moment all
discipline seems painful rather than pleasant, but later it yields the peaceful fruit of righteousness to those who have been trained by it.*

HEBREWS 12:5–11

CHAPTER 1

WHAT ARE
TRIALS?

I enjoyed athletics from my youngest days and played competitive basketball into my late thirties. Other than bumps, bruises, and sprains, I can't remember health problems of any kind. In my forties, yearly visits to Mayo Clinic were simply routine. At the end of my regular checkup in the fall of 2008 the doctor added these words:

"Your PSA (prostate-specific antigen) count has gone up again."

A review of the past four years revealed a pattern that finally got someone's attention. My count had gone from 1.3 to 1.8 to 2.2, then 2.7 and now was 3.1. Counts do fluctuate in men my age, but healthy men tend to have very low PSA counts. The regularity of this pattern had seemed significant to me, and I remember wishing the doctor had made a bigger deal about these counts earlier. But I also knew that PSA counts aren't always related to cancer, but can indicate other, less ominous health issues like enlarged prostate.

My doctor was now saying, "This is a problem, we've got to check it out further."

That meant scheduling a prostate biopsy. The experience was somewhere between a punch in the face and dental work without Novocain. Having a robotic pincer shoot through the wall of the large intestine to collect dozens of tiny specimens of the prostate produces an experience of core-pain unlike any other. I kept hoping that the level of discomfort I was going through was an indication of the accuracy of the test.

When life is hard, it is for a reason. Do you know what trials are and do you know God's purpose for them?

Days later, I was taking a taxi home from the airport when I remembered I hadn't called to get the results from my test. *Just another matter on my to-do list,* I thought as I called the urologist.

I reached him by phone, and with few preliminaries he said, "You've got cancer."

Such a small statement with such large effects—life-altering. In retrospect, I think many of us actually live expecting "the other shoe to fall" at some point. We realize at some level that we are not exempt from potential disaster, and we tend not to wonder *if* but *when* and *how* our number is going to come up. Those of us who know we are on the fallen world merry-go-round know that we won't get through life without some turns in the difficulty spotlight. But when the switch is thrown and the blinding light of a diagnosis like cancer hits us, the next moments are surreal.

There I was, alone (the taxi driver didn't need to hear my announcement), speechless (I immediately found myself thinking, *Can this be happening to me?*), and dumbfounded (*What do I do now?*).

When I arrived at home, I was still alone. The kids were away and Kathy was visiting family in Canada. The other realities in my life clamored for attention. I had to prepare a message and be ready to deliver it. I concentrated on that immediate task. But I don't remember the topic of that sermon.

After church, I met with my kids who were in town and brought them up to date. It was hard to tell them, but I felt I needed to keep them informed. We prayed together, and I listened to my children trying to put their shock and trust into words before God. Kathy arrived shortly and I told her—I had not wanted to share news like that over the phone if I could help it. Then I got on Skype and talked to my daughter Abby, who was away at college, and let her know what was happening in her dad's life. Those were difficult moments for both of us.

Once my immediate family had the information, the news began to ripple through the congregation. Suddenly, twelve thousand of my best friends were responding, calling, and praying. Their desire to care for me was both comforting and yet also an added burden.

I began to look at treatment options (mentioned in the introduction). I learned the cure rate with radiation treatments is almost the same as the cure rate with surgical intervention, without surgery's significant risks. I looked into various kinds of radiation and eventually chose proton-radiation therapy. This is cutting-edge technology that is still not widely available (which explains our journey to California). By God's grace our insurance covered this method of treatment and the next phase of dealing with this challenge began.

As a subtext (and perhaps a central lesson) in this episode, all these events happened in the weeks leading up to a planned trip to Israel. This was to be Kathy's and my first time in the Holy Land. The medical people advised me that the treatments for cancer could certainly wait long enough to enjoy a true trip of a lifetime.

Our intimate group of 170 friends walked and worshiped together in the places where Jesus spent most of His time. I was reminded over and over that God's plans were far greater than my immediate problems. That week in Israel allowed me to get in touch with Jesus' power to heal and sense

His presence in an intimate way that built my faith for the months to come.

I discovered I had cancer in October. By the end of December, arrangements had been made for treatments in California. The study and sermons that led to this book began to take shape and an opportunity opened for me to preach in Pastor Greg Laurie's church near my treatment facility. If these lessons seem fresh, they are. I'm learning them and confirming them day by day in my own life.

RECOGNIZING TRIALS

As we lay a foundation for our study, let's establish some facts that you've just got to know about *trials.*

In the New Testament, the Greek word *trial* means to prove by testing; an event that demonstrates the genuineness of your faith in Christ and refines the quality of your spiritual life. So let's agree on this definition:

A trial is a painful circumstance allowed by God to change my conduct and my character.

My *conduct*—that's what I do. And then to a deeper level, my *character* —that's who I am.

Trials are about what God is adjusting in the actions I choose, and what God is doing to the character that helps me choose those actions. Several biblical terms for *trials* are actually interchangeable: *suffering, hardship, tribulation, chastising,* and *discipline.* Trials are hard times!

These hard times vary both in intensity and duration. Tribulation can take you by storm, fast and furious. Or a trial can stretch over months or years or, in some instances, decades. It can be small and irritating or huge and shattering.

The one thing we know for sure about trials is that everyone experiences them.

In fact, if you're one of God's children, you're going through a trial right now. Some size. Some shape. It is the most difficult aspect of your life: Is it physical? Is it relational? Is it economic? Is it emotional? Is it circumstantial?

A FATHER'S DISCIPLINE

Hebrews 12 is a great place to start answering our question "What are trials?" Read our Scripture passage on the first page of this chapter—better yet, open to this passage in your own copy of God's Word and track the flow of thought. Later you can write what you're learning in the margin of your Bible or write in the margins or the appropriate lessons in "Go for the Gold" (chapter 6) so you can return to these life lessons again and again.

Pick it up at verse 5b: "**My son, do not regard lightly the *discipline* of the Lord, nor be weary when reproved by him. For the Lord *disciplines* the one he loves.... It is for *discipline* that you have to endure.... For what son is there whom his father does not *discipline*?**" (vv. 5b–7, italics added).

Sometimes when you're studying a passage, you think to yourself, *I'm not sure what it's about.* No room for doubt here. The subject is *discipline*, a term that describes God's involvement in the hardest part of your life.

WHAT IS THE DISCIPLINE OF THE LORD?

The word used for *discipline* in Hebrews 12 is translated *teaching* in Titus 2:11, 12a, where it says, "**For the grace of God that brings salvation has appeared to all men, teaching us**" (NKJV). When our eyes are opened to the glorious truth that is found in Jesus, it is to *teach* us some stuff.

Discipline is training. It's instructing, like what parents do with their children.

DOES GOD SPANK HIS CHILDREN?

A couple years ago a TV network news program did a five-night feature on evangelicals. I just had to watch and find out what they think about me and my friends ☺. Well, as you might guess, they totally didn't get us. On Thursday night, they did a feature on "the role of corporal punishment in childrearing." Right—*spanking*. So they got this "expert" on childrearing that said, "Nothing good could ever come from causing a child pain."

Now I'm aware and sensitive to the horrors of child abuse, but step away from the excess and the evil and consider that statement in its rawest form: "Nothing good could ever come from pain." Really? Nothing? Like the birth of a child, or the renewal of a forest after a fire, or the signal that something is badly wrong in my health and needs to be attended to?

No good from pain? What about the salvation of mankind?

Fact: Pain is often a central part of God's purpose in this world. God *allows* and even *causes* pain in our lives. It's one of the tools He uses regularly to get stubborn sheep to greener pasture.

I'm fond of saying that "God's love is not a pampering love; God's love is a perfecting love." God doesn't say, "Here, Billy. Have some more cupcakes. Take the one with the extra icing." That's not God. Your grandma, maybe, but not God.

Are you saying that God spanks His children? Ah, yes, He does. The "expert" on the news program back-pedaled and said God only disciplined His children in the Old Testament. Well, welcome to Hebrews 12—**"whom the Lord loves He disciplines"** (v. 6 NASB).

For real! God spanks His children. He lifts the paddle and applies it with force in the hopes that the pain will bring us to an awareness of His deeper purposes. When He saved us, He started the process that He will continue till the day we die. Salvation is just the beginning. The only reason you're still here is because God is working on you. When His work's done, it's heaven for you, baby.

HAVE YOU FORGOTTEN?

Hebrews 12:5 asks a funny question: **"Have you forgotten the exhortation . . . ?"** In other words, *"Have you drawn a blank?"* "Where have you been?" If you look in your Bible, you see that part of the verse is indented, signaling that this is a quote from the Old Testament; Proverbs 3:11, 12 to be exact. Interestingly, this is the most frequently quoted Old Testament passage in the New Testament. Nothing else even comes close. Over and over New Testament authors quote this portion of Proverbs 3. No wonder then that the author of Hebrews asked, "Have you forgotten?" The writer is asking, "How could you not know this? This is critical information that cannot be neglected."

And here's the instruction: **"My son, do not regard lightly the discipline of the Lord"** (v. 5b). Don't think lightly of what God is doing. Go ahead and do some *heavy* thinking. A contrasting word is used nearby in Hebrews 12:2 in the familiar verse, **"Looking to Jesus ...who ... endured the cross, despising the shame."** The word *despising* is an antonym in the original language for the word translated here as *regard lightly*. Jesus *despised* the shame of the cross—He didn't regard it lightly. We can certainly be tempted toward shame in our trials, but we have Jesus' example to help us endure.

When God moves toward you to make some changes in your conduct and character, do not be casual or indifferent about His approach. Don't be sarcastic or blasé, *As if it really mattered,* or *I'm getting kind of weary of this,* or *I don't think God really knows my limits,* or the manifold number of nonsensical ways we communicate to God that we don't appreciate what He's doing in our lives. He's God! He's a Committee of One. He doesn't check with anybody and He knows what He's doing.

> DON'T BE . . . INDIFFERENT WHEN TRIALS COME YOUR WAY. IF THEY ARE NOT ALREADY HERE, THEY ARE COMING.

Don't take His work in your life lightly. Don't be flippant or casual or indifferent when trials come your way. If they are not already here, they are coming.

As an experienced pastor, I've seen the full scope of human hardship. No matter which part of those painful hardships is yours this moment, you cannot despise or regard lightly what the Lord is doing.

"Nor be weary when reproved by Him." The word *reproved* sometimes means *to convict.* The tone is intense, even harsh. When the goal is character transformation, God doesn't move toward you with kid gloves. He's coming in hard. He's taking it strong to the hole. You don't have to guess that He's around. Being reproved by Him is an intense thing; but we are not to be wearied by it as though nothing good was ahead. Over and over the Bible connects weariness and losing heart. When we are exhorted not to be weary, it is as if to say, "Don't get down about this. God has a plan, so keep looking up and expecting something good to come from this." When God comes toward you with something hard, that makes *life* hard, don't get down and give up, because **"the Lord disciplines the one He loves."**

Have you ever bounced a check? It's not a great day when that happens. You didn't have the money to cover the purchase to begin with and when the bank sends the check back, it has a fine attached! Good luck collecting on that. It's a circular problem, since one notice just follows another.

A TRIAL IS LIKE A BOUNCED CHECK . . . A PROBLEM THAT YOU DON'T HAVE THE RESOURCES TO SOLVE.

First of all, it's embarrassing because you didn't have the resources you thought you did.

It's frustrating because they tack on those extra NSF (not sufficient funds) charges.

It's difficult because you've got to work it out with the bank and work it out with the merchant. The whole thing is a huge hassle.

A trial is like a bounced check. You feel stuck with a problem that you don't have the resources to solve. The temptation is to rant to God: "Do you see me over here, God? Do you see that I don't have what it takes to get through this? Are You paying attention? I'm about to bounce a lot of checks here. I don't have the resources. I don't have it emotionally. You're rattling my faith, God. Don't leave me in this mess."

Those expressions of desperation you feel so awful about are in fact the exact truth that God has been trying to bring to your attention. You flat out *don't* have the resources. He wants you to come to the place where you get before Him in a deeper way and tell Him what's He's known to be true all along: you are in way over your head.

God is taking you to a new level of dependence, and He *knows* what He's doing.

WHY DOES THE LORD
DISCIPLINE HIS CHILDREN?

Why does the Lord discipline me? Verse 6 says, **"For the Lord disciplines the one he loves."** Well, there you go. He disciplines you because He loves you.

You might be tempted to think, *Well, if You loved me, God, you wouldn't leave me over here with empty pockets and bounced checks.*

Let's get a better concept of love before we go on. Far from abandoning us when we're going through difficult trials, God moves toward us. Far from folding His arms; God is rolling up His sleeves. He's getting ready to do something in your life that you haven't previously been willing to let Him do. And He moves *toward* you. Isn't that good news? God is moving *toward* you. In fact, trials are proof of love. That's the point our Scripture is trying to teach us.

Never forget this: The motivation for God's action in allowing your life to become so hard is love. He *loves* you. His eyes are upon you. His attention is toward you. All of His thoughts are about you. The goal of all your pain is your restoration to a deeper sense of His love. But keep in mind that this is biblical love—a love that is willing to take you through a valley to get you to a hilltop. No pseudo solutions or quick fixes with God. He is going for change in you at the deepest and most lasting level.

I was blessed to have great parents. But they'd be the first to admit they weren't perfect. One time when I was eleven years old, my brothers and I were playing basketball at a schoolyard, maybe a quarter of a mile away from the house. Suddenly one of those summer storms came up and KA-BOOM!—huge thunder and lightning, and the rain poured down. Now, to an eleven-year-old, this was all swweeeet. Basketball in the *rain.* But our dad was home alone, terrified for us. I get it now. *Look at it outside. My boys—where are they!?*

So first he was fearful, but not for long. Quickly fear turned to anger, and all I remember is before we ever got in the front door, he already had his belt off. I've teased with him about this, and how over the top he was, but now that I am a dad, I totally get it.

Here's what you need to know. God never does that. God never disciplines His children in anger. He's never like, *Sorry, guys, I kind of lost it for a minute. Is everybody okay?* God never loses it. With surgical precision, God orchestrates the details of our lives and perfectly measures good and difficulty, blessing and discipline.

We need to be careful about the analogy here. As human parents we have a lot of our own stuff tied up in the way we train our children and because we need things from our kids too. We get fearful or tired or insecure, but how much does God need? *Well . . . nothing.* God doesn't think, *I've just got to get some of these feelings out and I'm not sure how to handle it.* He doesn't *have* any needs and we're certainly not meeting His needs. He loves us perfectly and unselfishly. God's discipline is not from self-interest.

> HERE'S WHAT YOU NEED TO KNOW. GOD NEVER DISCIPLINES HIS CHILDREN IN ANGER.

He's indifferent to what the neighbors think of His children. He's not afraid of what will happen if we don't learn. He won't say, *I've got to get this into you or what's going to happen up ahead?* God's not getting some sense of fulfillment through who He makes you into.

But I thought that all of this is for God's glory. Yes, it is. But do you think God is sharing His glory because it jazzes Him? Do you think God is up in heaven saying, "Well, it was a great glory day today. We hit some new numbers?" No!

God wants us to glorify Him because that's what we were created to do! God's pleasure is in Himself, not in us. He loves us and so everything that He does is for our good and for our benefit. Even the fact that it brings *glory* to Him is something that He's sharing with us.

Then notice, **"and chastises"** (another word for *discipline*). It's unfortunate and weak that the NIV translates that word as *punishes*. There is no punishment in discipline. All of the punishment for your sin was placed upon Christ at the cross. God is not punishing you. The goal is your benefit, nothing else.

IS IT A TRIAL OR A CONSEQUENCE?

Let's freeze-frame for a second and make a really important distinction about trials. Always try to ask yourself this question, *Is this a trial?* or *Is this a consequence?* Many times people say, "We're going through the most awful trial right now!" yet a discerning person would want to say, "Uh, I don't think *that's* a trial; that's a consequence for your own actions."

For example, you lost your job and money is tight, so you rob a bank. You end up in prison with a mean cell mate. Do you call that *trial* or *consequence?*

Don't be thinking, *God is refining me.* No, you probably shouldn't have broken the law.

Take a hard look at your situation because the way out is different if it is a consequence. The way out of a consequence is repentance. If you did wrong you need to make it right with God through repentance and with the people your sin injured through restitution.

A trial is a completely different scene. You didn't bring a trial into your life. This is something that God has allowed. You didn't cause it, you didn't choose it, and you could do nothing to stop it. Remember: A trial is a painful circumstance allowed by God to transform my conduct and my character. God Himself allowed that into your life.

> TRIALS WE EMBRACE AND LEARN FROM, CONSEQUENCES WE REPENT AND TURN FROM.

Now I understand that the lines may not always be perfectly clean in this distinction. Just keep in mind that the part you caused through a bad choice you made is resolved through repentance. *Trials we embrace and learn from, consequences we repent and turn from.*

"God is treating you as sons" (v. 7b). So, if you're reading this and thinking, *All this talk about trials is interesting but everything's rocking in my house, and it's been like that for a long time. No real problems of any kind. Everything's great with my family. My kids are perfect. I got money in the bank. I just came back from the doctor and he said I'm a finely tuned machine, etc.* Hate to tell you, but that's not good news for you, because all God's kids are getting it. If you have no trials in your life at all, not ever, you need to return to "Go." You may not really be part of God's family through faith in Christ.

The possibility may shock you, but if you have never experienced trials, you may be outside His family. But move beyond your surprise—you can repent and allow God to include you in His family. Here is a sinner's prayer that can help you walk through the steps of repentance:

Dear Father in heaven,

I know that I am a sinner and deserve Your rejection and punishment. Thank You for loving me enough to send Your Son, Jesus, into this world to die as payment for my sin. I repent of my sin and turn to You alone for my forgiveness. I believe that You are the only One who can cleanse me and change me. I now receive Jesus as the Savior and Lord of my life.

Thank You for coming into my life and forgiving me of all my sin. Thank You for giving me the gift of eternal life! I trust in You alone. In the name of Jesus I pray, amen.

If you prayed that prayer honestly and intentionally for the first time, you are now among God's children. And you can now look for Him to treat you as His child.

"It is for discipline that you have to endure. God is treating you as sons" (v. 7). When He disciplines you, God is relating to you as His own children. You can't just wake up one day and go, *I think I'll be one of God's children today.* Everyone is not God's child, no matter what you hear on *Oprah.*

John says that the only people who have the authority to be God's children are those who have received Jesus. **"To all who did receive him, who believed in his name, he gave the right to become children of God"** (John 1:12). I hope you've made that life-changing decision.

"If you are left without discipline, in which all have participated, then you are illegitimate" (v. 8). *Illegitimate* actually means "born of a concubine." *I don't know who your dad is, but it's not God the Father.* If you're not getting the discipline **"in which *all* have participated,"** you need to take a closer look at your heart and your hope. How could the Scripture be clearer?

> GET THE FULL BENEFIT FROM THESE TRIALS. LIFE IS SHORT AND ETERNITY IS VERY, VERY LONG.

As much as I appreciate this proof of sonship, sometimes I wish I didn't have this stuff going on in my life. Yes, I understand. Honestly, at times things seemed easier before we came to Christ. In a sense they were.

But in another sense, they were not. You were so clueless then. You didn't get the whole picture. You didn't know where you were going. You didn't know the big answers for anything. Life is harder, but now you have some categories. There's no question that the sons of this world have it easier for a season! But then, if they don't come to faith in Christ, it soon goes *really* downhill. What a sad and tragic end awaits those who reject Christ—God's only provision for their salvation. What a glorious thing to be called a son or a daughter of the living God through faith in Jesus Christ.

Part of being in the family means that God is now working on you. And life is so short; we will only be here for a little while longer. Whew! It's going by fast, isn't it? Get the full benefit from these trials. Life is short and eternity is very, very long.

YOU ARE LOVED

Do you remember the classic *The Adventures of Tom Sawyer*? Tom didn't have parents, but he had Aunt Polly. One day, Aunt Polly disciplines Tom. She pulls out a cane and begins to spank him intensely. As Tom wails, Huckleberry Finn is off on the side rolling around laughing. He thought it was great that he wasn't getting in trouble. But turn the page and Huck Finn is off on his own weeping as he realizes that he doesn't have anyone who cares enough about him to provide the security and the support that will make him better. It's only the silliest of children who dream of a life without discipline. "Lord, forgive us for the times that we have resented or even thought lightly of Your discipline in our lives."

Why does the Lord discipline His children? Because He loves us.

"Besides this, we have had earthly fathers who disciplined us and we respected them. Shall we not much more be subject to the Father of spirits and live?" (v. 9). "Earthly fathers" means literally, "fathers of the flesh" or dads. In New Testament times most everyone had a dad who showed interest in their training and development. Sadly, we have an epidemic of fatherless children in our culture. However, there are no fatherless children in God's family.

"We have had earthly fathers who disciplined us and we respected them." We respect our earthly fathers. *Respected* literally means *it turned us around.* I was going along thinking that I had everything together and then my father reached out and took hold of me to turn me around. Most of the time, when someone who loves us intervenes that aggressively we "respect" them, or turn around. We stop the wrong direction we were headed and set out in a better one. That's respect. We *had* to. There weren't a whole lot of ways out of that.

Dad was in charge! "You're going to learn this. You're going to sit here. You're going to study now. You're going to eat that!" *He's dad!* The older I get the more I realize how little I knew when I knew it all.

God, with infinite knowledge, moves toward us and He wants us to turn around. For that turning to take place two things must happen:

First, we have to admit, "You're right, God. I'm not." God is a perfect parent who uses perfect methods in the perfect amount. You get the logic. If you respected the discipline of an imperfect parent with imperfect methods, who used imperfect amounts, can't you respect the discipline of a perfect parent who uses perfect methods in the perfect amount? Can't you admit that God's right?

You say, "Well, James, I've got to be honest with you. I don't always feel that. Sometimes I feel like it's too much." I've felt that. My wife and I have felt that. "Not more, God. Not now, God." That's the way I felt when I found out I had prostate cancer. That's the way I felt when I learned my mother was very sick. "Do you see over here, God? We're just barely hanging on and do You think this is a good time for that?"

Sometimes chastening *does* overwhelm us. The reason is tied up in our reluctant and progressive admissions, as we resist and rebel:

1. *"There's no problem, God."* We won't admit we have anything that we need to work on. "I mean, have You been in my small group lately, God? Those people need You more than I do. Seriously, God. Work on them."

2. *"Okay, there's a problem. But it's not my problem."* We tell God, "It's my spouse's problem. It's my kids, God. Do you see the whole picture? You always come at the end, but did You see what really happened?" When we deny that the problem is us, we are refusing God's discipline and we get overwhelmed because we are attempting to get through it without His grace (a lot more on that in chapter 4).

3. *"Okay, there is a problem. And it is me, but it's not my fault."* Guilty with an explanation, but hardly an admission. "Now God, I'm sure You know about my past [or my parents or my _____; you fill in

the blank]." Sadly, some people have spent a lot of money talking to trained people whose specialty is teaching you to hang the blame in someone else's locker instead of putting the responsibility in the only place that can really benefit you—in *your* locker.

Nothing good is coming until I admit, "It's me, God. I'm the one. I'm the reason. You know what You're doing. I'm not making excuses, I'm not blaming others, I know the only person I can help is me. So let's get it on, God. Please help me get this in the rearview mirror as soon as possible, I really want to change."

And then, after we fully admit, we must do one more thing to turn around . . .

Second, we have to submit. **"We have had earthly fathers who disciplined us and we respected them.** Shall we not much more be subject to the Father of spirits and live?" For *subject to,* some of the translations have *submit.* Isn't it cool that God is called the "Father of spirits"? God is the Author or the Creator of the immaterial part of you—the part of you that lives forever. More than anything else, the part that He's working on is your spirit.

How should I respond to the discipline of the Lord? First, admit. Tell God, "There's a problem and it's me." And then I should submit to God. I should bow my knee to Him. "Do it, God. Do it in me. Do it to the max. Do it now!" Just get those things going and you have already turned the corner on trials.

Now let's talk about what to expect as you make those two choices.

THE RESULTS OF THE LORD'S DISCIPLINE

Here's a good summary of our imperfect human parents: **"For they disciplined us for a short time as it seemed best to them"** (v. 10a). Mom and Dad had only a few years and they did the best they could.

We put our youngest on a plane back to college today. I can't believe how quickly our kids have grown up. When they were young, I had like eight game plans I could use to train them. I had a whole deck of cards with moves I could make to teach them. On any given day, I could pull out two or three different cards and teach them in different ways. Now that they're in college, I'm wondering what happened to my cards. The time and the opportunity are gone! The human parenting experience passes so quickly and we discipline "as it seemed best."

Even the best parents don't have perfect judgment: It depends on the messenger—which parent is talking. It depends upon their mood—what's happening at work, or the marriage, or the weather. It depends upon the moment—there is so much subjectivity that goes into parenting.

But not with God.

1. His Good for Us

God **"disciplines us for our good."** This trial is working together for your good. As tough as the hard place you are at is, God is getting you to a better place. You have to hold on to that. God knows where the bull's-eye is and He's aiming for it. Like the best dentist, God is only drilling out decay, stuff that has made you restless and miserable all your life. When the work is done, your life will be better, but only if you embrace what God is doing. So get on God's agenda and embrace His good purpose as an expression of His love. Open your heart to His love, even in this. Open your mind to the incredible benefit that He will soon reveal.

And by the way, it's a specific good God's going after. He has something very precise in mind. Satan, your enemy, deals in generalities. He accuses you with vague insults, "You're such a loser." *In what?* "In everything." And so you walk around feeling like a complete zero. But that's your enemy talking. God never does that. God's is very precise in what He does in us. "We're going to work on *this* now. Ready? I don't like the way you talk to your wife . . . after work . . . on Fridays."

God's very specific. Satan condemns us with generalities. God lovingly moves toward us with surgical precision: "This is what's next on the sanctification agenda for you." The ultimate objective, of course, is *for our good.*

After forty-five weekdays of treatments in California, I returned to the Midwest to wait for results. Waiting four long months to get a read on the success or failure of a course of treatment takes on its own form of agony. Week after week of "not knowing" might have been unbearable except for two powerful, strengthening factors. The first was a growing sense in my day-to-day interaction with God that things were going to be okay—He had things in hand and under control. The second was the unexpected reality that there were more pressing matters at hand to distract me from dwelling on my health.

I remember a number of times sympathetic friends came to me: "You must really be burdened with the uncertainty of your cancer treatment."

My response was, "Oh yeah, there is *that,* isn't there?" Pressing matters had moved my focus from mere waiting and pacing, but those thoughts were always in the back of my mind.

Now I realize I was on an accelerated learning curve in the area of trials. I was getting a new sense of God's seriousness about sanctification in my own life.

2. His Holiness for Us

"That we may share his holiness." *Holiness.* Usually when you use the word *holiness,* people roll their eyes or wince. *Holiness? That's it?* This proves that we don't get what holiness is yet. Holiness and happiness should be synonyms. Holiness is the complete state of God-centeredness and God-likeness. Sin causes suffering. If you choose to sin; you choose to suffer. Holiness is the absence of everything that causes turmoil, pain, restlessness, and fear.

You definitely want more holiness, and that's what trials are for, **"that we may share his holiness."** Your holiness is God's endgame in the matter that caused you to start reading this book in the first place. Okay? So here's the next important question . . .

HOW DO I MAKE
THE MOST OF THE LORD'S DISCIPLINE?

Wouldn't you agree with Hebrews 12:11? **"For the moment all discipline seems painful rather than pleasant."** Not a lot of explanation is needed there. The problem is that trials often give me nearsightedness. I can only see what's right in front of me and I miss what's coming *later.* **"But later it yields."** If you plant submission to God in your life there will be a great yield or harvest up ahead. If you plant resistance and rebellion to God's will for your life, that will result in a very different harvest.

What's coming? **"the peaceful fruit of righteousness** [a synonym for holiness] **to those who have been trained by it"** (v. 11). In the chapters ahead we are going to talk a lot about how to be trained by a trial and what happens if we refuse, and what about trials that go on and on, etc. But for now let's just review the main parts of this first portion of Scripture. To make the most of the Lord's discipline, remember these three things:

1. *The pain is momentary.* This is not going to go on forever. Better days are ahead.
2. *The profit is immense.* You will receive **"the peaceful fruit of righteousness,"** the practical quality of godly living—a bushel of blessing, a barn full of bounty.
3. *The promise is conditional.* The profitable fruit of righteousness comes **"to those who have been trained by it."** That's what we're going for in this study. Your trial can train you for righteousness. I hate the thought that I'm wasting my time here or going through this pain for no purpose. Pain has a good purpose—don't you want to get it right this time?

Prayer of Commitment

God, I want to be trained by this trial. I want to experience the peaceful fruits of righteousness. I want to be a partaker of Your holiness. Thank You that You know the way that I take. Thank You that, by Your grace and by Your Spirit You promise that when You have tried me, I shall come forth as gold. I'm counting on it. I'm resting in it.

Thank You for it now, in Jesus' name. Amen.

FROM GOD'S HEART TO MINE

Hebrews 12:5–7

My son, do not regard lightly the discipline of the Lord, nor be weary when reproved by him. For the Lord disciplines the one he loves, and chastises every son whom he receives. It is for discipline that you have to endure. God is treating you as sons.

Hebrews 12:11

For the moment all discipline seems painful rather than pleasant, but later it yields the peaceful fruit of righteousness to those who have been trained by it.

MINING FOR GOLD

1. Pause over the prayer at the end of the chapter and wait in silence for God to speak to you. The first few actions or decisions you make following each of these chapters will make a huge difference in your life.

2. As you think of your life in the light of this chapter, what have been some trials you have experienced? Which are the obvious ones in your life right now?

3. How clear are you on the difference between trials and consequences? Too often we jump to the conclusion that we're bearing a cross when we're actually suffering the consequences of poor choices.

4. Have you settled the issue of ultimate consequences between God and you already by submitting and admitting your condition as part of sinful humanity? When did the sinner's prayer become your personal prayer?

5. How does God's love as a perfecting love rather than a pampering love affect your view of trials?

6. What signs can you point to in your hard times that indicate God is moving toward you for good?

7. To what extent are you willing at this point to "be trained" (Hebrews 12:11) by God through your hardships?

*But **he knows** the way that I take;*
when he has tried me, I shall come out as gold. Job 23:10

God Sees

He knows the circumstances I am facing.

God sees you on the road you are walking today. He sees the steps you must take today to get through this hard place. Proverbs 5:21 tells us that **"a man's ways are before the eyes of the Lord, and he ponders all his paths."** This means that God not only watches the winding of your road today, He is also thinking about every step and everything you must step over. WOW! God is considering your next fork in the road too, the good choice and the dismal misery-inducing one. Your Father in heaven is reflecting about what you are going to decide. Even though He has known from eternity past every detail of your life, He is still meditating upon it as it plays out. That blows me away.

God knows the way that you take. He wants you to succeed in the testing you are experiencing. Considering His great love for you, do you honestly think He would let you go through more than you can handle? No. He won't let this hard season knock you off the path of your highest usefulness to His kingdom. And He wants to help you make sure you don't drive yourself off that high road.

God is near to you when your heart is broken, and saves you when your spirit is crushed (Psalm 34:18). God draws near to you during a hardship unlike at any other time in your life. Maybe this is why the desperate need comes. Maybe this is the very moment that God is seeking to engineer— the moment of your turning as never before to Him.

If this is your moment and you don't know how to pray, God even knows that. Romans 8 tells us that God's Spirit prays for us when we don't have words. Just start praying and sharing your heart. Thank God that He knows the way you take.

Count it all joy, my brothers, when you meet trials of various kinds, for you know that the testing of your faith produces steadfastness. And let steadfastness have its full effect, that you may be perfect and complete, lacking in nothing.

If any of you lacks wisdom, let him ask God, who gives generously to all without reproach, and it will be given him. But let him ask in faith, with no doubting, for the one who doubts is like a wave of the sea that is driven and tossed by the wind. For that person must not suppose that he will receive anything from the Lord; he is a double-minded man, unstable in all his ways.

JAMES 1:2–8

CHAPTER 2

WHY
TRIALS?

Glen Chambers had a heart to serve God on the mission field. He got his Bible training, raised his support, and was filled with all the anticipation of serving Christ as a missionary. On June 23, 1959, he arrived at the Miami airport to board his plane to Bogota, Columbia, with a connecting flight to Lima, Peru. He was so excited! As he waited for his flight, he wanted to write a quick note to his mom. He didn't have any stationery, so he grabbed a newspaper from the floor of the airport terminal and tore off a section from one page where there wasn't a lot of print. He wrote his letter, folded it up, and dropped it in the mail slot before his plane took off.

The plane landed in Bogota and Glen soon boarded for his final destination. His Avianca Airlines flight reached cruising altitude, but before it began its descent, the plane crashed into the 14,500-foot Cerro Baco mountain, along the coast of Peru. There were no survivors.

After the funeral on July 1, Glen Chambers' letter was delivered to his mom. As she opened the envelope and unfolded the note, all she saw was the word "Why?" It turns out that the newspaper corner that Glen had torn off to write his note on—in the center of it, printed on the page—was one word: "Why?"[1]

Why? It's the question that hits the hardest.

It's the question that hurts the most.

It's the question that lingers the longest.

It's the question that every follower of Jesus Christ has asked. You've asked it and so have I. *Why, God?*

When life is hard,
the first light at the end of the tunnel
is insight into why
God has allowed this to happen.

Does your heart pound a little faster reading that question? Is your secret exposed? Have you been quietly anguishing, even pleading with God for some answers: "*Why this, why me, why now?*"

BEFORE WE CAN GO ANY FURTHER . . .

You've got to put this question to rest before we go on. The good news is that God does provide answers in James 1. But before those truths can take root in your life, you must ask yourself, *Am I willing not only to* hear *God's answers, but to* embrace t*hem?* I want you to get full benefit from these truths; nothing will sound right until you first settle this with the Lord. So take a moment right now, put a bookmark on this page, get on your knees if you need to, and ask the Lord for help.

Promise yourself and the Lord that nothing is off limits; that any "why" will be okay as long as it is the truth. Tell God that you want to know what He is seeking to accomplish in your life no matter what that "something" is.

If you're *not* willing, then tell that to the Lord, too. Say, "God, it's too hard. I don't see how I could accept certain answers. But Lord, I can't go on like I have been, so *I'm willing for You to make me willing.* Here I am—change my heart."

By praying these difficult prayers first you will be in a lot stronger place to get the benefit from what you are enduring so you won't have to come back this way again.

MY CHURCH TRIAL

Welcome back. As we get ready to look at the remarkable truths of James 1:2–8, let me share one of my greatest trials, which happened early in our church ministry.

This memorable ministry test happened to me while I was already on staff in a wonderful church in the Chicago area, with an interim plan to stay there for another year after graduation from seminary. As graduation approached, we received offers for ministry in well-established churches from Winnipeg, Canada, to Sarasota, Florida. Right in the middle came a phone call from a group of eighteen people in a suburb nearby. "We've just come out of a prayer meeting," they said, "and we believe God wants you to come and start this new church with us."

Not interested. Now that I had been to seminary, I was eager to preach to a congregation on a weekly basis, and the idea of starting from scratch with a handful of people held little attraction for me.

I listened to the spokesman for the group, but I had little intention of taking this any further. Yet as I hung up the phone, for one of the few times in my life I felt a spiritual heaviness come over me. I sensed God saying, *Don't laugh about this.*

So Kathy and I knelt down by the couch in our little seminary apartment. Our prayer was something like, "Lord we told You we would go anywhere and if going anywhere actually means staying right here, then we are willing to do that." After that prayer, our next step was to meet with the group who had called.

What followed was a unique and memorable experience of listening to people who enthusiastically, warmly, and clearly articulated all that we had been hoping and praying for in a church. They wanted a church with passionate and unapologetic preaching of the Word of God. A church where fervent prayer was fostered and expected. They vividly pictured a thoroughly contemporary church without theological or cultural compromises. As they talked, Kathy and I looked at each other and without speaking knew these people were describing exactly the kind of fellowship we had been longing to be part of in ministry.

Kathy and I left that meeting knowing we had to definitely include this opportunity on our list of open doors. Eventually it became clear, and I gave them the news: "Kathy and I are in. We'll do this with you. We're going to start this church together."

As a young pastor in a seed-church, we didn't have two dimes to rub together, yet people gave generously of time and other gifts. The original group helped us in so many practical ways. We found a location for the church. We planned an informational banquet and then launched the church. Within eighteen months our starter group of eighteen people had grown to four hundred regular attenders.

That kind of church growth in a large northern city was amazing for the time. People were coming to Christ every week. These new believers were also taking rapid spiritual steps and developing into faithful disciples. They, in turn, were inviting others who were often drawn by the remarkable changes they were witnessing in their friends' lives. The signs of God's work were all around us. And yet there were also growing signs of resistance and painful reminders that God was doing His work despite flawed materials.

One of the leaders of the original group who invited Kathy and me to come gradually became a source of relational trials. He was a successful self-made businessman and deeply committed to Jesus Christ. But as the church grew, a factor in his makeup became clear; he was used to having his own way. He expressed this characteristic by increasing efforts to assert control. Emergency board meetings became a staple of my pastoral life. There were "issues" that needed airing on an almost weekly basis.

Many of the complaints and concerns were not only unhelpful input—the music is too loud; the service too long; the tone not right—they were also presented in an unhealthy and critical way. I was a twenty-eight-year-old pastor experiencing the painful erosion of my role. The constant challenges and undermining were hurting me deeply. I wasn't sure what to do, but I needed a break from the weekly routine of crisis meetings.

> I WAS A TWENTY-EIGHT-YEAR-OLD PASTOR [AND] THE CONSTANT CHALLENGES . . . WERE HURTING ME DEEPLY.

This was the end of April, 1990. We had a special guest at our church who, in the context of worship and freedom, assumed that some less-than-traditional aspects of her theology would be accepted. She shared a testimony that was quite alarming to many in the leadership of the congregation, particularly the founding group. They arrived at the conclusion that since I had extended the invitation to this speaker, I must approve of all that she had shared. Instead of considering that I might be as upset as they were and like-minded with them in wanting to prevent any misunderstandings, they moved toward a frenzy of concern over the orthodoxy of my own theology. As-sumptions led to accusations and suspicions. In the minds of the leadership team of the church, something had to give.

Meanwhile, I had left town for a much needed break with my brothers. Back home, high-level discussions were held. And although the church finances were precarious at the time, the leaders decided to spend church money to fly me home a day early so that the serious issue could be resolved. The associate pastor and I appeared before the board that was clearly bent on "having it out" once and for all.

As they began to innumerate the concerns, I had to agree with some of them. Their comments did help me see that I was still naïve as a young pastor, and I tried to listen for the valued counsel in their words. I did what I could to counter and correct the misunderstandings over teaching. But I was also struck by the level of anger in the chairman of the board. The Scriptures have guidelines on how to handle an angry man, and when the board was finished presenting their concerns, I turned to the leader and attempted to gently confront the deeper issues of his anger. Clearly, he was not accustomed or prepared to be addressed in this way. His almost immediate response to my effort was to get up and walk out.

Soon the news came that he had not only walked out of the meeting; he had left the church. We made several concerted attempts at reconciliation, but he was adamant in his stance. Behind the scenes there was a furious phone campaign and our congregation of four hundred shrank almost instantly to two hundred and fifty. By the time the dust cleared, I realized that twelve of the original group of eighteen who had planted our church were gone.

Those days were devastating. The loss of those relationships hurt in ways I can't describe. To live through the growing pains of a young church suddenly seemed an awful lot like the dying pains of an imploding dream. Kathy and I had never wavered from our heartfelt desire to stay in one place and serve God for the long haul, but we suddenly knew a lot better what that commitment was going to cost us. This was the first big test of our commitment.

Now let's look at James 1:2–8.

CONSIDER YOUR TRIALS . . . *WHAT?*

I'd like to nominate James 1:2 as one of the most outrageous statements in the Bible.

"Count it all joy, my brothers, when you meet trials of various kinds." Count it all . . . *joy?*

That is what James wrote, through the inspiration of God's Spirit, but it doesn't add up from our perspective. Getting a more biblical definition of joy really helps us make sense of the encouragement to find joy when life is hard. Joy is something very different than what we commonly refer to as *happiness*. So when the Scripture says, "Count it all joy," the Lord is not saying, "Be happy about your trials."

Happiness is something completely different. Happiness is circumstantial. Happiness is based on happenings, I've heard said. It's an in-the-moment, *Oh-I'm-so-excited* kind of feeling.

Here's a story to illustrate. When our kids visited Kathy and me while we were living in California during my cancer treatments, we thought it'd be fun to go see the taping of the television game show *The Price Is Right*. I won't tell you the whole—hilarious—story (you can watch a clip from the show on whenlifeishard.com; get ready to laugh), but during the show I was reminded in my front-row seat just how fleeting this whole idea of human happiness is.

The contestants on *The Price Is Right* stood no more than two feet from us and no matter what was being bid on, they went ballistic! When household appliances were paraded in front of us, they screamed, "A washer and dryer!? Aaawwww!" I wanted to ask, *Don't you already have one of those?*

It was crazy and such a James-1 reminder that "Count it all . . . joy!" has nothing to do with happiness. We're not talking about that fleeting, circumstantial, oh-I'll-be-so-happy-if or won't-it-be-great-when emotional highs.

JOY COMES ONLY FROM GOD

You can't make yourself joyful. Joy comes only from God. When James says, "Consider it all joy," he's telling you, "Reach out to God. Get God's heart in this matter."

So what is joy? Here's a definition: *Joy is a supernatural delight in the Person, purposes, and people of God.*

Have you ever sensed God at work in you, or seen His obvious hand in a situation and knew in your heart of hearts that *God did that!*? Have you ever stood on a moonlit night by the shore looking up into space and sensed your soul being eclipsed by the God who made it all? What you felt in that moment was joy in who God is.

Joy is also something we exchange as brothers and sisters in Christ. As I write this I am at a place called Camp of the Woods in the Adirondack Mountains of upstate New York. I am with about two thousand people I have never met and know almost nothing personal about. Day after day, as I present these messages, I sense such a oneness of heart. We all have the same Master, we all follow the same book, we all have the same Spirit living within us. How could I have such a moving, connected, wonderful resonance with people I do not know? It's called joy.

Have you ever been in a worship service where with one loud voice you felt caught up in proclaiming the awesome majesty of God? Something is happening inside you and it's more than singing—that's joy! All of these things produce such joy that it makes "come on down and bid on (drumroll) a *newww carrrrr!*" seem kind of trivial and pathetic, doesn't it?

A supernatural delight in the purposes of God means you know there's something bigger than yourself going on here. There's something unfolding that is so far beyond the here and now. God has a purpose. Joy in trials says, *I'm going to find a way to trust Him even though I'm not seeing Him.*

JOY IS ONLY FOR THE FAMILY

That's why James 1:2 says, "Count it all joy, *my brothers*" (italics added). Only Christians get to experience joy. I hope you're a follower of Christ and that you have made the decision to turn from your sins and embrace Christ for forgiveness. Only a follower of Christ would ever consider a trial joy, because if life is only about here, now, and my happiness, trials really don't make any sense or give any good. If you're not a believer in Christ, and if all you are living for is the next fifteen minutes, then unfortunately your fifteen minutes of happiness is almost over and you would have good reason to resent a fly in that ointment. But those of us who are committed to a higher more eternal purpose really can get our thinking to a place of joy no matter what. Here's how . . .

ADD IT UP

Time to Count

The most important word in James 1:2 is *count*. Some translations use the word *consider*, which in some ways makes the meaning clearer. It's literally the idea of *press your mind down upon this*. Weigh your trial; measure it; calculate it; put it in perspective. That's part of *counting* or *considering* it joy. We must recognize why we're here. "I'm not here for grins. I'm not here for my ego. I'm not here for my pleasure or even for my family. I'm here for God!" If you're a follower of Jesus Christ, that is the only reason you get to draw another breath—for God.

The life of a true Christian is about displaying the superiority of the life lived in God. That's why Christians get cancer. That's why Christian parents have prodigals. That's why Christian businesspeople go through bankruptcies. The contrast is deep between how a son or daughter of the kingdom and how a son or daughter of this world handles hard times. Ask a doctor if he or she has witnessed any difference between a Christian parent who runs into the emergency room holding a dying child and an apparent heartbroken happiness-seeker facing the same nightmare? They will tell you the difference is like day and night.

Whatever you are facing as you turn these pages and look for wisdom, right here—in this moment—your situation is your opportunity to shine the light of Christ to those who observe you. You can display the superiority of a life lived in God. Realizing that reality and embracing it with your whole heart allows first a sprinkling of joy . . . and then a stream and finally a *downpour* to flood your soul.

But you can't come to that conclusion coping on your own. You can't consider it joy when you're filling your face with food to dull your pain. You can't consider it joy when you're filling your mind with entertainment to dull that pain. You can't consider it joy when you're filling your heart with anger to dull that pain. And you can't come to the joyful conclusion when you're filling your body with substance to dull that pain.

Only by considering why you are here, and what life is really about and where you will be going very soon can you consider your trial joy. Paul said, **"For our light affliction, which is but for a moment, is working for us a far more exceeding and eternal weight of glory"** (2 Corinthians 4:17 NKJV).

A Bit of Homework

You say, "Okay, James, I want to get off the pity party and back on the joy train but practically how do I do that?" I can only tell you what I have done to keep this focus. It involves preparing four 3 x 5 cards. (Don't just think about this bit of homework. Do it.)

Get four 3 x 5 cards (you can also print these cards at whenlifeishard. com) and write the following on them:

- On the first card, write: WHAT HAPPENED TO ME? Write down the details of your trial.
- On the second card, write: WHY AM I HERE ON EARTH? What's the purpose of my life according to God's Word?
- On the third card, write: HOW CAN THIS TRIAL ADVANCE THAT PURPOSE? What can I do today to advance the purpose of displaying the superiority of a life lived in God?
- On the fourth card, write: WHAT RESOURCES CAN I ACCESS THIS MOMENT TO HELP ME? If you're a follower of Christ, you are one of God's children and have the strength and the comfort of the Holy Spirit within. You have the Word of God giving wisdom to direct your path

That fourth card is key. Your resources extend beyond the Holy Spirit and the Word of God. You also have available supportive Christian relationships. You have the grace of God, which allows you to begin again when you have failed. And you have this book, written by someone who has endured a lot, learning lessons along the way to get beyond this hard place. And ask yourself, *How can I draw down upon those resources to make God-honoring choices and find my way through this trial?*

Then keep going over these cards so that God's purpose in your life will not be lost. This is a practical exercise toward the goal of being able to "consider it joy."

A PHRASE AT A TIME

"Count it all joy ... *when you meet* trials" (v. 2, italics added). The New King James Version translates "when you meet" a little bit better: "when you fall into." Because that's how it happens, right? "I was going along. Life was just rockin' out, then BAM! I was flat on my face. I did not even see it coming!" Is that how it's been for you? That's been part of the pain for the MacDonalds—people we trusted, circumstances we couldn't see, events beyond our control and ... surprise! But here the Word of God is just so honest and true to reality.

"Of various kinds" (v. 2b). In the Septuagint, the Greek translation of the Old Testament, *various kinds* is the same phrase that is used to describe Joseph's coat of many colors. Our trials are very different. My trials are different from yours. Some trials are tough and some are tragic. Some are difficult and some are devastating.

Watch out for the temptation to think, *I wish I had her trial!* It's never helpful to compare God's work in others to what He is doing in and around you. To do so is to question God's wisdom in what trials He allows into someone else's life. That is a very bad plan. Don't get between the hammer and the work on that one. Just leave other people's situations with God and focus on what He is doing in you.

"For you know that the testing of your faith produces ..." (v. 3). If you don't know it now, you *will* know it tomorrow. Trials separate the men from the boys. Trials separate the sheep from the goats. Trials separate the wheat from the tares. The proof of whether you are a true follower of Christ often comes with trials.

When life is hard, you discover whether you're really in Christ or just an imposter who showed up for a sunny day at the beach. Matthew 7:20 declares, **"By their fruits you will know them"** (NKJV). One of the fruits of a genuine believer is that you endure hardship. You continue. You don't give up. **"He who endures to the end will be saved,"** Jesus said in Matthew 10:22 (NKJV).

Defection is proof of a false conversion. John said in 1 John 2:19 (NASB), **"They went out from us, but they were not really of us; for if they had been of us, they would have remained with us."** When the heat is turned up, false believers run in a hurry. That's why I thank God for Bible-teaching churches that actually deepen people's faith. Otherwise when trials come, a lot of people who have been served pep talks from smiley preachers will bolt for the exits. They didn't lose their salvation; they never had it as their response to hard times testifies.

THE FAITH TEST . . .
AND THE FAITH FINAL EXAM
About the Faith Test

"The testing of your faith" (v. 3). A trial is a test of your faith.

I hated tests in school. I was way smarter than the grades I got. I remember going into those tests completely stumped. *No, I don't know the answer to this question. I don't even understand the question.*

I still don't like tests, but I understand why they are important. I've come to see that being tested by God is very loving. Frankly, I'd rather find out now that I don't have the real thing than get to heaven and be surprised. You want your faith tested. You want to put your full weight down on the faith that you have in Christ and see if it holds you up, because *if your faith hasn't changed you, it hasn't saved you. Better to find out while there is still time to get it right.*

Take the Faith Final Exam

Testing is God's good plan to get some good results. **"For you know that the testing of your faith produces..."** You have to take the faith final exam over and over in your life. I'll give you the three essay questions up front:

1. *Do you believe that God is in control?* (Please support your answer from Scripture.)
2. *Do you believe that God is good no matter what you see, no matter what you face?*

Trust me that I understand the gravity of the first two questions. God is trying to get you to the place where you pass the test, where your faith can answer these questions correctly. It's a difficult process. No matter what happens, do you believe that God is in control? Do you believe that God is good and has your best interests at heart? Do you believe that what He allows is for His good purpose?

Here's the final question:

3. *Will you wait on Him by faith until the darkness becomes light?*

Will you wait? If you say, "I'm not seeing it right now," then you get an A for honesty. But do you believe God is in control? Do you believe that He is good? Are you willing to wait by faith until you see His goodness? Because you *will* see it. Now or later—you will see the goodness of the Lord.

Psalm 27:13 has meant so much to me: **"I would have despaired unless I had believed that I would see the goodness of the Lord in the land of the living"** (NASB). "My trial would have overwhelmed me," the psalmist said, "unless I had believed." But I *do* believe it. I believe that I will see the goodness of the Lord and not just in heaven but *in the land of the living—* right here on this earth. While I'm drawing breath in these lungs, I will be able to sum up all that has happened, and I will say, "Somehow in it God has shown His goodness."

Take the test, and if you pass with flying colors, your life will be immeasurably better.

TRIALS' GOOD BENEFITS

You say, "Okay, so my hard times are testing my faith, but what benefits do they bring me beyond a confidence in my conversion?"

1. Trials produce staying power

"Count it all joy, my brothers, when you meet trials of various kinds, for you know that the testing of your faith produces **steadfastness**." Testing produces *steadfastness* . . . or *patience* (NKJV) or *endurance* (NASB). The most important word to understand regarding trials is the Greek word *hupŏmĕnō*, from two words: "*mĕnō*" means to "remain"; and "*hupŏ*" means "under." The testing of your faith produces the ability to "remain under." That's what God's going for. God wants to give you the ability to remain under.

When you're under a trial you feel the pressure. You feel the weight of whatever it is that God has allowed, but if you were to tell the full truth right now, what do you want most when a trial comes? "I want to get out from under it."

When my child is rebelling, I often don't want to be a parent anymore. When our church's construction project was way over budget and I feared I would lose it all, I didn't want to be a pastor anymore. When my friends were betraying me and breaking my heart, I wanted to hole up and hide from everyone. The thing we most want to do when life is hard is jump ship, but staying put is the very thing God wants to teach us most.

This is key: If God can get to you the ability to remain under the pressure, He can give you every other good thing He wants for you. All the character qualities God wants to pour into your life are coming through the funnel called "remaining under." He wants you to stick with it, hang in there, and under NO circumstances give up.

But remaining under is the last thing I want to do, I tell myself. It hurts! It's hard! I have fears. I can't take this much longer, God! When a child rebels; when a spouse betrays; when a sickness threatens; when my heart breaks into so many pieces I can't even find them—I want this over! But quitting cuts exactly against the grain of what God's trying to accomplish in me—and you.

Okay, we have been studying James 1:2–4 for insight into why God allows life to become so hard sometimes. And so far we have learned that a supernatural joy is to be our focused thoughtful pursuit when trials surprise us because it's a test that produces the ability to stand strong through which God can get us everything else

> *I WANT THIS OVER!*
> BUT QUITTING
> CUTS AGAINST
> THE GRAIN OF
> WHAT GOD'S TRYING
> TO ACCOMPLISH.

He wants to give us. So why don't more people "remain under" the trials they face?

We surveyed 100 people, asking them to "name something you want to do instead of remaining under your trial." Here are the top four answers on the board to this question:

1. "I want to complain." We may stay under the pressure, but if we do people are gonna hear about it. We're gonna sound off from sunup to sundown about all our feelings and frustrations. That's not remaining under. That's not what *hupŏmĕnō* (the noun form) means.

2. "I want to lash out." We take it out on the people around us. We take it out on our spouse (or kids), on our roommate, coworkers, or best friends. Anyone who dares to get close is in danger of catching shrapnel from our verbal assault. We're hurting, so they are gonna be hurting too. *That's not remaining under*—That's not what *hupŏmĕni* is.

3. "I want to bail." We tell ourselves, *I am so out of here. I didn't sign up*

for this. That's not why I became a Christian. That's not why I took this job. That's not why I got married. That's not why I became a Mom. I don't have to take this! The worst possible decision we can make is to bail when the burdens get too big, but it's the thing we want to do most. That's not remaining under. That's not what *hupŏmĕni* is.

4. "I fold under the pressure." Those responding this way say, in effect, "Crush me, God! Here I am! Take me out! Run me over, God, I would rather be dead than be under this pressing weight another moment."

It's not right to think those thoughts, but I have to be honest and say that I have had them in some of my darkest moments. Giving up and folding under the pressure is no way out either. *That's not remaining under.* That's not what *hupŏmĕni* is.

> INSTEAD OF GETTING BETTER, PEOPLE WHO REFUSE TO REMAIN UNDER GET BITTER.

That's what we'd rather do. But what should we do when the pressure is on and life becomes very hard? The apostle Peter tells us, **"Humble yourselves, therefore, under the mighty hand of God so that at the proper time he may exalt you"** (1 Peter 5:6). This is a critical word for you who are in a very hard place.

Remain under the pressure by God's grace and in His strength and when you pass the test by persevering, a lot of great things are in your future.

Why remain? Because the nail that doesn't remain under the hammer will never reach the goal; because the rough diamond that doesn't remain under the chisel will never become a precious jewel; because the gold that doesn't remain under the fire will never be a thing of beauty; because the Christian who doesn't remain under the hand of God will never see His purpose for the trial accomplished and will never experience the blessing on the other side. Instead of getting better, people who refuse to remain under get bitter. You must know someone like that who "when the going gets tough the tough get . . . going"—on their way anywhere, somewhere but right here, under the mighty hand of God in joyful submission to His will and His way for them.

Question: Will you remain under this trial and wait for God to accomplish His purpose in your life?

2. Trials produce life transformation

"And let steadfastness have its full effect, that you may be perfect and complete, lacking in nothing" (James 1:4). I played a lot of basketball back in the day. I sprained my ankles many times and I learned too late that the best way to handle all that black-and-blue is to fill a wastebasket with ice, and top it off with water. Then, while the injury is fresh, put your wounded foot deep into that cold water and leave it there.

If you can last for one minute, it's just crazy painful. But if you can keep it in there for two minutes, the injury and its recovery time will be cut in half. (The problem is that after two minutes the pain is so excruciating that you will be saying words your mother didn't know you knew.)

If you can hang on for two and a half minutes, you can be playing basketball again by Thursday, but the pain of holding your foot in that arctic water will have you crying out for someone to bring you a sharp object. Even with my worst injuries I seldom made it two and a half minutes.

But here is the incredible thing about "remaining under the pain" of having your foot in that cold bucket. If you can hang on for three minutes, you'll be walking on it tomorrow. The pain will be consuming those last thirty seconds, worse by far than the injury itself now. But you will walk tomorrow.

It is just that way with trials. You can come to the place where the circumstance itself is less painful than the commitment not to give up. If staying put was easy, if submitting to what God allows and not giving up was simple . . . everyone would be doing it. The fact is, most Christians are going round and round with God about the very same things because they change scenery or marriage or job or church rather than remaining under the trial and letting God change them.

I had to learn that in my cancer treatments. Every morning, day after day, I got up early and drove down to the hospital and submitted to a very humbling process. I couldn't talk about it when it was happening, but a five-inch rod with a balloon on the end was inserted "where the sun don't shine," and the balloon was inflated with six ounces of water. The purpose of this was to reduce collateral damage to other vital organs by pushing them out of the radiation area. I knew what was happening, I knew why it needed to happen, but it was tough just the same to submit to that process forty-five times, plus the practice round. Uncomfortable, painful, humbling, and more, but I was reminded every moment with every sight and sound and smell that my cancer was serious and life-threatening and that I didn't know what the outcome would be.

> WE THINK THE ANSWER IS A NEW ENVIRONMENT WHEN THE REAL ANSWER IS A NEW ME.

But I trust God. And I remain under His hand—persevere—when everything in me wants to cut it short and run. They said this treatment will take forty-five daily procedures, to which I want to say, "Oh yeah? Well, I'm on treatment number 41 and I'm tired and I want to go home. Number 41 out of forty-five is fine. I want to be done with this. I'm hurting . . . and I miss . . . and I don't want to be here anymore and do this even one more day."

What a perfect scenario to test my faith. Do you see it? Don't you want to say to me, "No, James, remain under. Bear up in God's strength. Don't cut the process short or you'll never see the good." Thanks. Yes, you're right. And now six months later I have the good test results to prove the healing is well under way and I am so thankful I didn't yank my foot out of the bucket when it was hardest not to. Do you feel the same pressure to cut-and-run in your life?

We think a change of scenery will fix the problem. Spouses leave their marriage and then they are shocked to find their same problems in the next marriage!? "You remind me so much of my first wife!" Well, duh, the same guy picked his second partner. Meanwhile, a pastor leaves and moves to a new church and is dumbfounded to find the same problems with different faces. Why? Because the pastor is part of the problem too, because he didn't stay put and learn the things God wanted him to learn. We think the answer is a new environment when the real answer is a new me.

That's why God has you working in the place where you can do the most good; in the mirror. God is working on you and me from the inside. God is trying to change you and grow you on your own customized training program. Only as you keep your foot in that bucket for as long as possible will you notice the good result.

Let me give you another chapter in the story of the ministry trial I included earlier in this chapter. After the successful businessman and mover in our church had walked out, we continued periodically to make overtures to him, seeking reconciliation. God continued to do good work on him (and certainly me). The process was painful and time-consuming. By the time this man was on his deathbed, he and I were fully reconciled.

Given the history of all that happened, our reunion continues to remind me that God's healing power goes far beyond the physical aches and pains that often become the focus of our prayers. The ailments that touch our souls get his special attention. Remember, Jesus looked at the man who was obviously so immobilized that he had to be lowered by friends on a mat, through a roof. He obviously needed physical healing, but Jesus saw the man's deeper, truer need. So Jesus administered an effective dose of forgiveness. The fact that the man walked home with his mat was simply one of the side benefits to the priceless gift of reconciliation with God.

Years later, the son of that man is one of the best leaders at Harvest Bible Chapel. The evidence of genuine reconciliation never stays between two people; it opens ways for God to do amazing things in all our lives.

WISDOM FOR TRIALS

Convinced? I'm guessing your faith is growing and you're feeling a bit hopeful that your trial is for a purpose. You can feel that *hupŏmĕnō* rising in you, strengthening your will to stay under the pressure as long as it takes because you love the idea of being changed. The problem that remains is that you have some questions you are gonna need answers to. As in: "God, I was pretty sure I was gonna bail, but now that I have decided to hang in there I have some things I need to understand a bit better." The biblical word for this is wisdom, and God wants to give it to you: **"If any of you lacks wisdom, let him ask God, who gives generously to all without reproach, and *it will be given him"*** (James 1:5, italics added).

James 1:5 is one of the most abused verses in the New Testament. I'm guilty too. When I was in college, I'd stay up all night and goof around. Then I'd go to the exam the next day and desperately pray, *Oh God, You promised that if we lack wisdom, that we're just to ask. And if I've never asked before, I'm asking now! Please give me wisdom on this test right now!* Sorry—no wisdom is coming. James 1:5 was not intended as a crib note to bypass study.

The context of this promise as we have been learning is trials. God promises that if you will ask for wisdom *in your trials* that He will give it to you. If you humble yourself before the Lord, and say, *I want to know why You've allowed this trial. What are You trying to teach me, Lord, and where can I begin to work on myself first?*

The "Why" God Answers

God doesn't answer the "existential why," as in, "Why do bad things happen to good people?" I think there are some good answers to that question, but that's not what this is about.

God doesn't answer the "ultimatum why," as in, "You had better tell me why this is happening right now, God." (Like you're going to intimidate Him?)

God doesn't answer the "observation why," as in, "Why doesn't my neighbor have to go through this, God?"

The "why" that God will answer is the "personal why." "Why did You allow this in me now, God? What do You want to teach me?" You get to Him with that. "If I remain under here, God, what are the things that You want to work on? What's next in Your plan of transformation for me?" God answers that "why" in a hurry.

God is not playing poker. He *wants* you to see His cards. He will flood your life with wisdom when you ask for the kind of information He wants to give you. "Why am I like this, God, and why has it been so hard for me to change? Why have I not been able to see this, and so stubborn when others have pointed it out to me? Why have I been so slow to realize the price I have paid and how this flaw in me has injured others?" These are the "whys" of trials that God longs to answer. These are the cries for wisdom God generously supplies.

He also will answer that prayer **without reproach** (v. 5), which means that He won't sink His teeth into you for asking. He will answer you generously. If you come before God with, *What are You trying to teach me now, God?* He's not going to say, "You again? Don't you know how many things I have to do up here? Do you know how far down the list you are in order of importance? Quit bothering Me with your little questions about your trials." God's not like that. He loves you.

One of the greatest moments between you and the Lord is when you come to that place of submission and He takes you in His arms and soothes your soul and binds your wounds and fills your mind with wisdom for what's ahead. Tell the Lord you want to know. "Here I am, God. I'm not going anywhere, but I don't want to have to learn this again. Help me learn this right now."

Ask without Doubting

Tell God this, and He will answer you generously; He will not reproach you. But here's the key: Make sure you really want to know.

Notice what James 1:6 says: **"But let him ask** [for wisdom about why this trial has happened] **in faith, with no doubting, for the one who doubts is like a wave of the sea that is driven and tossed by the wind."** Ever watch a beach ball in the crowd at a sports arena? It floats here, then gets batted over there; then it drifts up or down. Now it's over there.

A lot of us are like that in the middle of a trial. You sort of want to know what God wants to teach you, but you've got these creeping doubts: "Okay, God. I'm ready to hear what it is. But before You start, could I read off the things that it can't be? You can't ask me to keep loving my son." Or you tell God, "You can't ask me to put up with my boss at work. I'm just not willing to face up to my materialism and lack of compassion for the poor. I just can't do it!"

Up and down, tossed with the wind and waves. Nothing's coming to that doubter.

"For the one who doubts . . . **must not suppose that he will receive anything from the Lord**" (vv. 6–7). If you doubt, you're just "like a wave of the sea that is driven" (v. 6). You've got no more control over where your life's going than that beach ball. Someone says something to you and you are encouraged; and then, oh no, you hear someone else's words and now you're discouraged. Now I'm on; now I'm off. I love God, but I'm also bitter. You might be living that exact life because you're not in true submission to God in the midst of your trial. Believe me, I know what I'm talking about.

Instead, each of us must humble ourselves and say, "God, whatever You want to teach me—nothing is off limits. Take it all! Say anything, God. I don't want to have to come back this way again." Only when I pray for wisdom with no strings attached, no limits of any kind on what God can talk to me about, can I expect the wisdom I need about the why of what's been so very hard.

You and I have got to ask in faith.

We've got to really want to know. You can't have anything crossed off the list. It doesn't matter how long you've rationalized it or excused it or pushed it away.

"For the one who doubts is like a wave on the sea that is driven and tossed by the wind. **For that person must not suppose that he will receive anything from the Lord**" (v. 6–7). If you don't really want to know what God wants to teach you, He's not going to answer. "I keep asking Him for wisdom, but He's not telling me." He will tell you when you *really* want to know. You have to ask in 100 percent openness to whatever God wants to do in you, no doubting allowed.

DOWN WITH DOUBLE-MINDEDNESS

James tells us that a doubter is **"a double-minded man, unstable in all his ways"** (1:8). Someone who doubts is like a two-souled person—a person who's like, "I want what God wants, but I don't want what God wants. I want to learn, but I'm angry!" I can think of a lot of times in my life where my focus in a trial was less on what God was teaching me and more on how hurt I felt by the actions of another. When my focus is on revenge, or making my point, or hurting you back, or getting the pressure off, I am very unstable—not just in the trial but in everything.

All right, ready to commit to *hupŏmĕnō* —to remaining under the trial? Ready to pray the real "why" prayer about the person in the mirror, the only one you can really change? Then pray the prayer of commitment that follows.

Prayer of Commitment

As best as I know how, God, I'm humbling myself before You. I'm bowing here in Your presence and I'm saying, "Lord, I do want wisdom and nothing is off limits. Whatever You want to teach me, I want to learn."

Why has this come into my life, God? You could have prevented it, but You've allowed it. Why have I not been able to learn this until now? Show me my weakness and sin as it really is. Open my ears to the words of those who love me and have tried to help me see it.

Forgive me for focusing so often on how others are getting it wrong and what they need to learn. Show me just myself, Lord, and let Your work in me be enough . . ."

Nothing is off limits. By faith, I'm asking You for wisdom—for insight into the next gap You want to fill between who I have been and who You want me to be. I pray for Your glory to be seen in my life as never before. I want to be that person with staying power. I'm not going anywhere. I'm not quitting. With Your help I will not give up. By Your grace, I choose to remain under the pressure until You choose to release it. What do You want to change in me, God? Please show me now . . . [Get your pen ready and begin to write down all faults and shortcomings the Holy Spirit reveals to you as a result of this study of James 1:2–8].

By faith, I ask You to do this work in my life. Hold me here in this place until it is done. I trust You and I love You. In Jesus' name, I pray. Amen.

FROM GOD'S HEART TO MINE

James 1:2–4

Count it all joy, my brothers, when you meet trials of various kinds, for you know that the testing of your faith produces steadfastness. And let steadfastness have its full effect, that you may be perfect and complete, lacking in nothing.

James 1: 5–7

If any of you lacks wisdom, let him ask God, who gives generously to all without reproach, and it will be given him. But let him ask in faith, with no doubting, for the one who doubts is like a wave of the sea that is driven and tossed by the wind. For that person must not suppose that he will receive anything from the Lord; he is a double-minded man, unstable in all his ways.

MINING FOR GOLD

1. Look again at the prayer that ended the chapter. Take time to make it your own expression of wanting God's perspective on the trials He has allowed into your life.

2. How did you respond when you read the following statement in the chapter: "Tell God you want to know what He is seeking to accomplish in your life"?

3. How do you recognize joy when you see it or experience it?

4. In what ways are you using the companion cards suggested in this chapter?

5. How did you do answering the three questions of the faith final exam?

6. In your trials, would you say your tendency is to look for patience in God's lesson or to look for a way out? Why?

7. How is this study helping you focus on the crucial importance of remaining under discipline?

But he knows the way that I take;
when he has tried me, *I shall come out as gold.* Job 23:10

God Measures

This trial is for a season.

Clearly stated, trials have a season. Whether for weeks or months or years, the normal trial lasts for an appointed time. Job 23:10 says that *"when he has tried me,* **I shall come out as gold."**

In my own trials, I have come to see that a lot of the struggle is about when. Sometimes we think, *If I knew now what the outcomes would be, even if they are not all exactly as I desire, I could begin to deal with it.* But if we are walking by faith and resting in the promises of God, we don't have a lot of questions about what. We know what God has promised to do—His intention is to bring good out of any trial. So the only thing left to be burdened about is the when. When will God act? When will God plead my case? When will God heal my body? When will God restore that relationship, or right that wrong, or . . . ?

When—that's what we most long to know!

Job 23:10 assures us at least that the time is coming. There's going to be an *afterward.* Hold on—there's going to be an end to this trouble. God is watching your life and at some point in this trial, He will say, *Enough.*

Job's assurance can be yours today. Get under it and don't waste any days. The sooner you and I get what He has for us, the sooner He will bring us out. This painful season is coming to an end. "When will He do that?" you ask. **"*When* He has tried you."**

Since therefore Christ suffered in the flesh, arm yourselves with the same way of thinking, for whoever has suffered in the flesh has ceased from sin, so as to live for the rest of the time in the flesh no longer for human passions but for the will of God. For the time that is past suffices for doing what the Gentiles want to do, living in sensuality, passions, drunkenness, orgies, drinking parties, and lawless idolatry. With respect to this they are surprised when you do not join them in the same flood of debauchery, and they malign you; but they will give account to him who is ready to judge the living and the dead. For this is why the gospel was preached even to those who are dead, that though judged in the flesh the way people are, they might live in the spirit the way God does.

The end of all things is at hand; therefore be self-controlled and sober-minded for the sake of your prayers. Above all, keep loving one another earnestly, since love covers a multitude of sins. Show hospitality to one another without grumbling. As each has received a gift, use it to serve one another, as good stewards of God's varied grace: whoever speaks, as one who speaks oracles of God; whoever serves, as one who serves by the strength that God supplies—in order that in everything God may be glorified through Jesus Christ. To him belong glory and dominion forever and ever. Amen.

Beloved, do not be surprised at the fiery trial when it comes upon you to test you, as though something strange were happening to you. But rejoice insofar as you share Christ's sufferings, that you may also rejoice and be glad when his glory is revealed. If you are insulted for the name of Christ, you are blessed, because the Spirit of glory and of God rests upon you. But let none of you suffer as a murderer or a thief or an evildoer or as a meddler. Yet if anyone suffers as a Christian, let him not be ashamed, but let him glorify God in that name. For it is time for judgment to begin at the household of God; and if it begins with us, what will be the outcome for those who do not obey the gospel of God? And "If the righteous is scarcely saved, what will become of the ungodly and the sinner?" Therefore let those who suffer according to God's will entrust their souls to a faithful Creator while doing good.

1 PETER 4:1–19

CHAPTER 3

WHAT TO DO WITH

TRIALS

Only loving deeply can bring you to this kind of desperation. A member of our family was in an awful relationship and all we knew to do was get in the car and drive. We got to St. Louis, five hours of thinking later, but no answers.

A sleepless night in some hotel I would rather forget and back in the car driving again. Where are we going? I don't know. When will we go back? I don't know. Why are we driving? Still no answers.

At one point I got a return call from a man I had never met who a friend of a mutual friend told me might have some answers. But after his greeting, I had no words. He asked me what was wrong, asked me for some details—an explanation for why I had tried to reach him. What came welling up from my soul surprised and embarrassed me as I clenched my cell phone to my ear and ducked behind a store. Convulsions gripped and contorted my chest as I bent over in anguish and sobbed into the phone, "I don't know what to do, I don't know what to do."

It took me several minutes to gain my composure enough to talk . . . I will never forget that day and though much grace has come since that moment I am altered by that suffering.

When life is hard,
stop and ask God,
"What do You want me to do?"

Have you been suffering? That can't be prevented, but you can have a better sense of what to do when it comes. Better than I had. That's what this chapter is about, but you must begin with a hard truth: Suffering is part of the Christian life. And if you weren't taught that, when suffering comes, it can blow a big hole in the side of your "toy boat theology."

"I DIDN'T SIGN UP FOR THIS"

What? Suffering? That's not what I signed up for! Suffering will come as a surprise if you bought into the Western World self-help Jesus, who came to build your self-esteem and maximize your human potential by Friday. That false message is just a cartoon, the invention of Jesus marketers seeking to profit from the power of Christ and His cross.

Welcome to the biblical gospel. We belong to God; our lives are not our own. We have been bought with a price. The earth is not our home; we're just strangers here for a very brief visit while we are seeking the city that is to come. Jesus suffered, the apostles suffered, and great men and women through every era of church history have been refined by their maker in the furnace of adversity. Following Jesus means suffering is the norm, not the exception!

That's why our next study is in 1 Peter 4:1–19. I want you to embrace the reality and know what to do when it comes, rather than being surprised and shattered by it.

1 Peter 1:1 was addressed **"To the elect exiles."** The original audience was people who had been sent away from their homeland because of their faith in Jesus Christ. They were homeless for Christ.

1 Peter 1:6 sharpens the picture of the exiles' situation; **"though now for a little while, if necessary, you have been** *grieved by various trials"* (all italics added).

1 Peter 1:10–11 lays the groundwork for God's including suffering in His plans; **"various prophets . . . predicted the** *sufferings* **of Christ."**

1 Peter 2:19 acknowledges the obvious unfairness of lots of suffering. **"One endures sorrows while** *suffering* **unjustly."**

1 Peter 2:20 even points to the injustice in some suffering. **"You do good and** *suffer* **for it."** And then, in rapid succession, note how Peter goes back-and-forth between the suffering of Christ and the suffering of those who believe.

> **Christ also** *suffered* **for you, leaving you an example.** (2:21)
> **When he** *suffered,* **he did not threaten.** (2:23)
> **But even if you should** *suffer* **for righteousness' sake.** (3:14)
> **Better to** *suffer* **for doing good for Christ also** *suffered.* (3:17–18)
> **Since therefore Christ** *suffered.* (4:1)
> **Beloved, do not be surprised at the** *fiery trial.* (4:12)
> **As you share Christ's** *sufferings.* (4:13)
> **Yet if anyone** *suffers* **as a Christian.** (4:16)
> **Let those who** *suffer* **according to God's will.** (4:19)
> **And after you have** *suffered* **a little while.** (5:10)

It's hard to miss the theme. You are probably suffering *reading* this! The key word in 1 Peter is *suffering.*

SUFFERING IN RELATIONSHIPS

Suffering comes in many forms, but I think one of the most painful is in our personal relationships. I have been writing this book while on a sabbatical from my regular duties at church. For twelve weeks I have had a chance to reflect, study, write, and seek refreshment, devoting a significant amount of time to tracing the events that got us to where we are today as a church. There is a growing body of history generated by over twenty years of adventures in ministry.

Harvest Bible Chapel fits into the category of large church, seeing hundreds of people converted to Christ and baptized every year. We have rejoiced over at least fifty other congregations planted in North America and around the world as part of the outreach of Harvest. But people tend to underestimate or downplay the kind of emotional output that is necessary and the imposing hurdles of various kinds that must be overcome along the way to abundant fruit for God. I have jokingly told more than one visiting group that I gave up my hair for this church. I am also very aware that the story of Harvest Bible Chapel represents, among a lot of other things, the crucible of my ongoing sanctification. God has blessed the perseverance that He continues to provide. I believe He has blessed the commitment to not waver regarding His Word. Everything good about Harvest Bible Chapel exists for God's glory.

What is not apparent to casual or quick observers are some of the underlying themes of pain that are woven into the fabric of our history. One of the persistent themes has been the disappointments with people. We have repeatedly preached and practiced the principle that there is no enduring relationship without forgiveness. When I first expressed those thoughts, I conceived of relationships in which I forgave others and they forgave me. The quality of relationship flows from the mutuality of forgiveness. And I have certainly seen that basic principle proven true in relationships that *have* lasted—mutual forgiveness is part of the tie that binds us. I have had the same associate pastor and the same personal assistant for twenty years. They and other leaders have signed on to the vision that we're going to do life together.

Along the way there have also been people who have said they were committed for the long run and who acted like they were in for keeps, but who didn't last very long. For them, "no enduring relationships without forgiveness" turned out to mean, *if I blow it, you'll forgive me and if you blow it, I'll go somewhere else.*

The reason that there can be no enduring relationships without forgiveness is because relationships exist in a world where we hurt each other all too often. But the suffering must be acknowledged and diluted with forgiveness, or the suffering of relational sin will prove too much.

SUFFERING WILL COME

The apostle Paul said pain would come. He told Timothy that **"All who desire to live a godly life in Christ Jesus will be persecuted"** (2 Timothy 3:12). *So who exactly does that "all" include?* It includes all of us.

That biblical warning comes from God's heart of love. If you're driving down the freeway and somebody cuts in front of you and you see a collision coming, you brace yourself. If you stumble down a step and start to fall, the first thing you do is put your hands out to break your fall. You brace yourself. And the reason God's Word repeats the fact that suffering is God's number one tool for chiseling our character is so that we can brace ourselves. He loves us, so He warns us.

Since suffering is coming (or for some of us, is here) you need to know what to do. As I look at 1 Peter 4, I see four very specific actions for us to put into practice during our trials.

WHAT TO DO DURING TRIALS

1. Guard Your Behavior

Let's start with the right mind-set.

Jesus paid a price for our sins. His death was an atoning sacrifice. 1 Peter 4:1 commands, **"Since therefore Christ suffered in the flesh, arm yourselves with the same way of thinking."** "Arm yourself" is a military term that means *get ready for battle.* Put your armor on.

How did Jesus think like this? If you read the Gospels, He was always talking about, **"My time has not yet come"** (John 7:6). Jesus knew from Moment 'A' where this was all going to end up. Forget that faulty idea that Jesus "ended up on the cross." He was in perfect control of every situation at every moment. Of course we understand that Jesus could summon **"legions of angels"** (Matthew 26:53) to rescue Him, but Jesus *went* to the cross. He turned His face to Jerusalem and headed there. He knew exactly what was waiting for Him there and He went anyway. He willed Himself to be our sacrifice.

We need to arm ourselves with the same mentality. My mind-set must be: *I'm going to get through this. This is my focus. I'm not surprised by it. God has this planned for me, so I'm staying under it!* I'm not scratching my head, asking, "How come I'm going through hard times?" I'm one of God's children and **"The Lord disciplines [those] he loves"** (Hebrews 12:6). Arm yourself with the right mentality.

YOU STAND AT A CROSSROADS AND EITHER GET BITTER OR GET BETTER.

Returning to 1 Peter, we're told, **"For whoever has suffered in the flesh has ceased from sin"** (4:1). This phrase has caused some real confusion. Some people say that this proves that Jesus was only sinless after He went to the cross. But the Bible is categorical about the fact that Jesus was without sin: He **"has been tempted in all things as we are, yet without sin"** (Hebrews 4:15 NASB).

Some people say that means that when I'm suffering I won't sin. Yeah, put that one in the *wish-it-was-true* category. Sadly, the opposite is more likely the case. Often when we're going through difficult times, we are more vulnerable to sin. You stand at a crossroads and either get bitter or get better. Either you're going forward and upward or you're going backward and downward. Trials present a watershed moment.

A better translation of **"For whoever has suffered in the flesh has ceased from sin"** includes the idea of *being restrained*. God desires that suffering would make you a better man or woman. He wants to use this in your life. Though temptation to sin can sometimes be heightened in trials, trials can make you more focused in your walk with Christ.

As I look through my journal over the last year, I see a seriousness that has come into my spiritual life. If there were things that I was not proud of lingering in the corridors of my life, they came to light. Pain in one area can sensitize you to other parts of your life. Suffering teaches you in new ways that life isn't a series of random unrelated events; it's all connected. As you formulate urgent prayer requests for issues related to your trial, you examine your life for anything that would prevent you from being heard. "Okay, God. Anything You see in my life that I need to deal with? Anything that I need to get right with You about? Any subject that I've not been listening to?" You get the mind-set of a warrior, not wanting to carry anything extra into the battle. Paul told Timothy, "Share in suffering as a good soldier of Christ Jesus" (2 Timothy 2:3). So arm yourselves with that mind-set.

"For whoever has suffered in the flesh has ceased from sin, so as to live for the rest of the time in the flesh" (1 Peter 4:1b–2a).

I love it where the Bible reminds us that life is not going to go on forever. Trials remind us that life is short. Ask anyone over forty-five and they understand. We're in a free fall. **"Our outward man is perishing day by day"** (2 Corinthians 4:16 NKJV). No matter the length of your earthly life span, you have only a few more years. James 4:14 says life is **"a vapor,"** and the further you get down the road and the more you've got in the rearview mirror—the faster it seems to go. Tick-tock, tick-tock.

GO HARD AFTER THE WILL OF GOD IN YOUR LIFE.

Back to our passage for great wisdom; "So as to live for the rest of the time in the flesh **no longer for human passions but for the will of God**" (v. 2b). God forgive us for the months and the years that we spent with our pleasure at the top of our agenda. What a shallow existence that was. Instead of pursuing personal passions, go hard after the will of God in your life.

God's will is God's Word. People ask me frequently what God's will is for their life. "Is it God's will for me to move to Topeka, Kansas?" Trust me on this: He doesn't care. He will still be able to do what He's doing here even if you're in Kansas and He will use you wherever you are if you're obedient to His Word.

God's will is for you to keep your commitments.

God's will is for you to be a person of integrity.

God's will is for you to be a hard worker.

God's will is for you to be a person of truth and sincerity and commitment to His way.

That's God's will.

Get all that done and then come back for more instructions. Here's more from 1 Thessalonians 4:3: **"This is the will of God, your sanctification."** God is incredibly interested in the kind of person you are. If you can be the *kind* of person God wants you to be, *where* you live is a lot less significant. So, Topeka, Kansas, may well be a great place for you to pursue God's will.

If you read part of verse 2, **"In the flesh no longer for human passions"** and thought to yourself, *"Yeah, I don't know if I'm completely done with human passions,"* pay attention to verse 3: **"For the time that is past suffices for doing what the Gentiles want to do."**

Remember the good old days? Yeah, in reality they were not that great. Think back to college. Or summer youth camp. Somehow, over time, we forget about the challenges of every season of life and we look back wistfully, longing for the nostalgia.

How about right now!? Newsflash: *These are the good old days.* Right here, right now, make the most of your life.

Look at the phrase, "doing what the Gentiles want to do" (v. 3). A foolish Christian would look back to their BC days (Before Christ), and think, *Now that I'm done with the sin thing, I wish I would have done a couple of* . . . Are you *kidding* me?

Does anyone have a list of what the Gentiles want to do? Actually, Peter made one. It begins immediately: **"living in sensuality"** (v. 4). The word *sensuality* means "a flagrant, unrestrained sexuality"; no boundaries; no shame. And then, **"passions . . . orgies."** The terms don't mean just sexual, though they definitely include that. Peter was referencing feasts where they would stuff themselves with food then make themselves vomit so they could eat more. And then repeat. Then repeat with alcohol and then vomit. And then repeat once more. **"Sensuality, passions"**—any pathetic memories coming to mind? The list goes on with **"drunkenness, orgies, drinking parties."** Then, notice the summary term, **"lawless idolatry."** All of this they did in worshiping false gods; it was part of their religion.

WE DON'T NEED A CONTEST TO DISCOVER WHO IS THE AMERICAN IDOL—IT'S EACH OF US!

You're like, *I would never do that.* Well, in the western world, the North American god is *you.* We do all these things in worship of ourselves. We don't need a contest to discover who is the American Idol—it's each of us! At least the ancient pagans knew there was a power bigger than themselves, even if they were making up a self-indulgent religion.

Verse 4 takes on special significance in the context of suffering. Guard your behavior: **"With respect to this they are surprised when you do not join them in the same flood of debauchery."** The word "flood" includes the idea of "being washed away by sin to a sudden, certain damnation." It's a flood of wickedness that rushes people into hell. Those who don't go with the flow of debauchery are singled out for special treatment: **"they malign you."** This is more than insults. The word in the original literally means they blaspheme you—"Bible-Thumper, Holy-Roller Jesus freak!" When it comes to joining the **"flood of debauchery,"** been there; done that. Just shame and regret, heartache and devastation in that ride.

Sin overpromises and under-delivers every time. It glitters, but it is not gold. It shouts for my attention. But it never gives me what it promises. Choose to sin; choose to suffer. Guard your behavior and don't go back there.

Worst of all, during a time of real hardship, you are a target. One chapter later, Peter warns that **"Your adversary the devil prowls around like a roaring lion, seeking someone to devour"** (5:8). Satan sees God's children when they're going through hardship and he's waiting for an opportune time to pounce on you. What God allows for your good, Satan wants to twist into evil. Sin that hasn't tempted you for a long time can *crush* you during a trial, when all of your strength and all of your resources and all of your energy are going into surviving! You're just trying to get by when Satan will come in and make a rush on you. You can find yourself stumbling and falling into thought patterns and action patterns that you thought were gone forever! *I never thought I'd touch that bottle again, but here it is—empty in my hands.*

Satan wants to shame you and grind you under his heel. He wants to take you back to square one and make you think you haven't made any progress at all. Listen, as a blood-bought son or daughter of the living God, you were born for something much better than that!

But do you want to know what to do? Do you want to know what to do during a trial? Guard your behavior. It's not the hardship but your response that really matters!

Eventually everyone will be judged for their actions. **"They will give account to him who is ready to judge the living and the dead."** Peter is describing the eventual judgment of the spiritually living and the spiritually dead. God is ready to judge or call to account both those who have life in Christ and those who remain dead in sin, for **"the wages of sin is death"** (Romans 6:23).

"For this is why the gospel was preached even to those who are dead" (v. 6). *What?! We don't preach the gospel to dead people, man!* Some churches teach that there is a second chance after you die to hear the gospel. The Bible doesn't teach that. Hebrews 9:27 teaches that **"It is appointed for man**

to die once, and after that comes judgment." One chance, one life. This is it. Yes or no. Up or down. Broad road or narrow road. Here's what that verse means: notice the tense in the phrase, **"For this is why the gospel *was* preached."** Present or past? It *was* preached to them when they were alive, but they're dead now. Peter is talking certainly about Christians who had died, but probably specifically those who had been martyred for the faith. The gospel had been preached to them. They heard it and responded and then they were saved. People called them forward and said, "Deny Jesus Christ or die!" and they chose to die rather than deny.

"For this is why the gospel was preached even to those who are dead, that though judged in the flesh the way people are, they might live in the spirit the way God does." At the end of the day, what matters most: a human verdict or God's verdict?

It doesn't matter who your mom says you are, who your spouse says you are, or who your kids or your coworkers or your crazy sister says you are.

All that really matters is that *I am who God says I am.* Even if you had to leave this world early because of some false verdict that was pronounced upon you. What an ultimate price a martyr must pay. But in the end, God's verdict is the one that will stand.

So, we have just seen that 1 Peter 4:1–6 tells us one crucial answer to *what* to do with trials: Guard your behavior.

2. Grace Your Relationships

Next, we head into some very practical instruction. **"The end of all things is at hand; therefore be self-controlled and sober-minded for the sake of your prayers"** (1 Peter 4:7).

"The end of all things is at hand." Here we are with the reminder again. Life is short. One way or another, we've got limited time.

"Be self-controlled, be sober-minded *for the sake of your prayers*" (italics added). We're in serious times. Laughter is one source of relief and it helps us drop our guard a bit. But we're on a topic as serious as a heart attack. This is not a time for goofing around. Even a kindergarten Christian knows that there's something incongruous about joking around with God. This is life and death. This is heaven and hell. This is about God's glory and Satan's kingdom in this world. This is serious business. So be self-controlled. Be sober-minded for the sake of your prayers.

And then notice this: **"Above all, keep loving one another earnestly."** I love that word "earnestly." When you get with the people you treasure, you want to take hold of them and love them earnestly. You are gonna put some energy into it.

Why are we loving earnestly again? Because **"love covers a multitude of sins"** (v. 8). Maybe you're thinking, *Well, not in my house. We don't cover anything, man! Everything's out in the open!* That's not super-loving. We all don't need to know about the sin that's going on in my house or where I work. Because I love these people, I don't want to shame them in front of you. I'm not going to parade their problems for everyone to see. Even as you rehearse some of your trials, don't go into hurtful details because you *love* the other people involved.

IF YOU'RE NOT SURE HOW TO LOVE, HAVE A PARTY. INVITE PEOPLE OVER.

That's the way we need to be in our relationships with one another. We don't need to pour out a big stream of *Do you know what my husband has done now?* And if you love him, you're going to cover that.

There's a bit of danger here; that doesn't mean you hide sin or that you put yourself at risk. If there are things going on at your house that are illegal, skip the "love covers" and just call the police. To someone reading this right now, that was your word of direction. If it's illegal, don't hide it under some Christian blanket that isn't really biblical. The authority structure in the church is meant to protect you when the authority structure in the home fails. Don't let some false spirituality promote sin in the name of a misplaced idea of love. But, apart from an illegality, love covers; it protects.

And then notice right in the middle of the trial context, **"Show hospitality to one another"** (v. 9). If you're not sure how to love, have a party. Invite people over from your church. *But I don't know anybody.* Well, meet some people. Stand in the lobby and give out cards. *But we're not really sure who to have over.* Well, have the wrong people over first. *Cleaning up my house and fixing a meal sounds like a lot of work!* "Show hospitality to one another **without grumbling**." Does God have you in mind?

The shortness of life and the importance of not complaining and acting out forgiveness have generated a personal plan. Kathy and I are going away in a few days and we have decided that part of our time will involve a big bonfire. We're going to take cards and write down the names of people who have deeply wounded us. We will make a record of relationships that have been marked with betrayal and deception. We can all agree that it is easier to forgive when someone comes back and says, "I'm sorry for what I did to you; I'm sorry for what I said to you; I was wrong in the way I handled that." But waiting for a gesture of reconciliation to happen is not healthy.

So, how do we go forward when those we forgive are unwilling to acknowledge they ever did anything that needs forgiving? We are going to take those name cards (prepared in chapter 2) and apply Romans 12:18 to them first, **"If possible, so far as it depends on you, live peaceably with all."** After we have confirmed that we have done our part in forgiveness and attempting reconciliation, we are going to give these broken relationships to God. Kathy and I are going to acknowledge that this is not a perfect world and there aren't any perfect people—certainly not us. We are going to offer those cards to God in the fire and agree that we are moving on. We are going to leave reconciliation of these broken relationships with brothers and sisters in Christ, in His hands and His timing.

As you read this account, it wouldn't help you if I included the names on Kathy's and my list. I'd rather invite you to think of the names on your list. Are there people who have hurt you that you haven't forgiven? Jesus left orders concerning what we must do. Are there people from whom you need to seek forgiveness? Neither waiting nor fearing is an acceptable excuse if we want to obey Christ. And are there people who continue to cause pain because you are hoping they will someday respond to the forgiveness you have offered them?

I can't think of a better time than right now to release those people into God's hands. If you find it impossible to release people you have forgiven, I would gently suggest that you reexamine what you mean when you say that you have forgiven them.

3. Give Away Your Gift

"As each has received a gift" (v. 10). Every follower of Jesus Christ has been given a gift. I believe that you get one gift. But think of it like a pie with several slices that enable you to serve God. For example, I got a big slice of leadership, a medium-sized piece of administration, another piece of exhortation, and a thin slice of mercy in my pie. You might say, "Oh! I've got a great big piece of mercy." Our pies are unique, with combinations of several ingredients. This is your gift. It's your capacity to serve God. Your gift is your supernatural enablement to make a difference in this world.

"As each has received a gift, use it to serve one another." Our gift serves not only our God but His people, especially during trials. So give away your gift in service. Please allow me to exercise my gift of exhortation and say, if you think your gift is encouragement or faith, be very submissive to the Lord when you talk to someone in a trial. Everyone who's been through a trial could tell you of somebody who said something that hurt. Thoughtless words, intended to encourage, can add significant pain.

But what should I say? Verse 11 will help. **"Whoever speaks** [during trials], **as one who speaks oracles of God."** You will never go wrong sharing Scripture. Avoid passages that may seem judgmental, but share verses from the Word of God that have meant a lot to you. Pour some of God's amazing grace into their lives directly from His Word. Send a verse in the mail. Send a verse by e-mail:

"Dear John: Praying for you. [Give reference, verse.] Love, Your Name."
Perfect! You're going to feed that person. You're going to bless them.
God's in charge of the trial. He needs messengers to speak for Him.

"Whoever speaks, as one who speaks oracles of God; **whoever serves**"
(v. 11). Share Scripture. Then, use your gift. If you're a server, serve. If you're
a speaker, speak. But whatever you do, do it **"by the strength that God supplies."** Be prayed up. Be filled with the Spirit. If you want to be used to bless
someone who's going through a trial, you need to be right with God. You
need to be drawing down upon God's strength. You will be saying, "Lord,
give me wisdom to know how I can help."

And here's our goal, **"By the strength that God supplies—in order that
in everything God may be glorified through Jesus Christ. To him belong
glory and dominion forever and ever. Amen"** (v. 11b).

I want to be used by God to help other people. As long as I am relying
on "the strength that God supplies," God can work "in everything" to bring
glory to Himself. I've seen this illustrated in my own life. When I told the
people in my church that Kathy and I were going to California for my cancer treatments, and that I would be teaching the series, "Turning Your Trials to Gold," many well-meaning people said, "Why don't you go out there
and just do nothing for these ten weeks? Just go get better."

I know what they meant and they meant well. I love them for the expression. But I had already come to understand that putting my feet up for
eleven weeks wouldn't be super healthy for me. It's healthiest to use your gift
in these situations. That's what's healthy for me—to be forced to dig into
God's Word myself so that I can draw down upon the strength that God
wants to give me. We're learning together about how to go through difficult
seasons. Use your gift.

What to do with trials?

1. Guard your behavior.

2. Grace your relationships.

3. Give away your gift.

And now the final exhortation.

4. Glorify God

The Westminster Confession says that the chief end of man is to glorify God and to enjoy Him forever. How does that translate to your life?

How old are you? The reason you got to be that age is so that you can bring glory to God.

Hoping to marry someday? Whoever you marry should be for God's glory.

Married already? Make sure that's for God's glory too.

Are you going to have kids? Make sure that's for God's glory.

Are you going to have a job? Go where you can glorify God.

Are you going to drive a car? Keep God's glory in mind.

That's what the whole life is about.

Remember, our goal is **"that in everything God may be glorified through Jesus Christ"** (v. 11b).

Glory is what emanates from God. The apostle John wrote, **"No one has ever seen God; the only God, who is at the Father's side, he has made him known"** (John 1:18). Nobody gets to see God. **"No man can see Me and live,"** God said (Exodus 33:20 NASB).

Remember Moses' bold request? He asked to see God's glory (33:18), and God said, "You can't. My glory would wipe you out. But tell you what—hide in this rock and I'll pass by and then you can see My after-burn. Because if you actually see Me, you'd be burning" (see 33:18–23). You can't see God and live. All you see is His glory. You see the manifestation of His presence; you see the evidence that He's around.

That unmistakable Presence is what the disciples sensed when they were with Jesus. John reported, **"And the Word became flesh and dwelt among us, *and we have seen his glory*, glory as of the only Son from the Father, full of grace and truth"** (John 1:14, italics added).

When Kathy and I were living in California, we'd take a walk every morning in the hills near our rental. We remarked every day about how beautiful the mountains were. **"I lift up my eyes to the hills. From where does my help come?"** asks Psalm 121:1. The answer follows, **"My help comes from the Lord, who made heaven and earth."** The psalmist looked at the creation and thought, "God!" Creation is shouting God's name, and God's glory (see Psalm 19). He created the universe to glorify Himself.

But here's the interesting point: The voice of creation will always be muted. The centerpiece of God's creation is us, mankind. We are here to display the glory of God. Do you remember what Jesus said? **"If these were silent, the very stones would cry out"** (Luke 19:40). The message of the existence of God cannot be silenced in the universe.

We're here to manifest God's presence. That's what your life is about from here on in. You can say with confidence, "I am here to display the superiority of the life lived in God. I'm here to do what the mountains do very poorly. My life is to *shout* the existence of God."

When you act this way, others will notice. "Look at her, how she goes through these trials. Look at how he triumphs no matter what! God must be in his life! Yes, He is."

That's why we're here—to glorify God.

RESPOND THE RIGHT WAY

"Beloved," in light of what you just read, **"do not be surprised at the fiery trial when it comes upon you to test you, as though something strange were happening to you. But rejoice insofar as you share Christ's sufferings"** (v. 12).

How practical! Don't be surprised when hard times hit—just do these four things:

1. Rejoice

"But rejoice insofar as you share Christ's sufferings, *that you may also rejoice and be glad* when His glory is revealed" (v. 13, italics added). If I'm living for God's glory, then when Jesus returns, His glory will be ultimately revealed. That will be the greatest moment ever! When He gets here, it's going to be awesome. **"The earth will be filled with the glory of the Lord"** (Habakkuk 2:14). **"Holy, holy, holy is the Lord of hosts. The whole earth is full of his glory"** (Isaiah 6:3).

"When His glory is revealed" (v. 13) will not only be true upon Jesus' return, it will also be true earlier—in the ongoing moment by moment in your trial as God's glory becomes apparent. You won't be able to help yourself—you will rejoice. Even though the trial may not be over, seeing a glimpse of God's glory in the middle of it will make your day!

2. Don't Be Ashamed

"Yet if anyone suffers as a Christian, let him not be ashamed" (v. 16). Don't be ashamed if you suffer hardship because you love God. Don't give up and don't stop talking about Him. Manifest the reality of God's presence in your life. Remember to have that mind in you that Jesus had when He **"endured the cross, despising the shame"** (Hebrews 12:2).

3. Examine Yourself

"For it is time for judgment to begin at the household of God" (v. 17). Look at your own life. **"And if it begins with us, what will be the outcome for those who do not obey the gospel of God?"** In other words, instead of getting up on my self-righteous high horse about nonbelievers, start with yourself. Ask, *How am I doing as one of His children who understands? Is my eagerness to find fault with others just a cover-up for my own shortcomings?*

"And 'If the righteous is scarcely saved, what will become of the ungodly and the sinner?'" (v. 18). It is only the grace of God that keeps you from falling into hell this moment. The only reason why the sun will rise tomorrow is grace. Grace doesn't just save you; grace *keeps* you. I hate the idea some have that, "I couldn't save myself so I came to the cross. But now I'm going to sanctify myself." No. Colossians 2:6 says, **"As you received the Lord,**

so walk in him." You couldn't take the first step without God; and you can't take any of the other steps without Him. You can't be successful in trials without Him. You can't do anything right spiritually without Him.

It's all of grace. That's what it means, "scarcely saved." You're just hanging on by the grace of God. If your self-examination doesn't leave you quiet, broken, and humble before God, it wasn't an effective self-examination. Do it over.

4. Trust Your Creator

"Therefore let those who suffer according to God's will entrust their souls to a faithful Creator while doing good" (v. 19). It's as if Peter is pulling us close together and saying, "Just get back to work, boys. Just keep going in the midst of trials. Don't quit. Don't give up. Don't stop teaching your class. Don't stop leading your home group. Don't stop sharing your faith. Don't stop reading your Bible. Just keep doing the things you've been doing."

Yes, entrust your soul to a faithful Creator. God is faithful, He's in control, and He's good. Decide now that you're going to wait until the darkness becomes light.

I receive great correspondence from people all over the world who are impacted by our Bible teaching ministry, *Walk in the Word*. As I was finishing this chapter, I received a letter from a proud grandmother. Sharol's attitude superbly illustrates the decision to "entrust your souls to a faithful Creator." I dare you to read it and not swell with faith by her example.[1]

Dear James,

During the past several months so many of your weekly devotionals have focused on the hard, unexplained tragedies that can cause us to worry, question, and cry out to God . . . *What? Why?* And *How??*

Our first granddaughter Simone was born with multiple unexplained birth defects from a "midline disorder" that gave her a pre-fused skull, deformed forehead, incomplete eye socket, deformed corpus callosum and thyroid, cleft palate, [and left her with] seizures and one kidney not working. Other than that, *she was perfect—a strawberry blonde, blue-eyed angel.*

She has had 10 surgeries in 20 months, many of them unplanned emergencies, where death was a strong possibility. In all this my son and daughter-in-law have remained strong, knowing God is in charge and loving Simone completely every day with joy!

So know that many times your weekly devotionals have helped me as we entrust Simone's life and health to His loving care, not knowing what, how, or why. There sometimes is no final answer, even though people ask me to explain.

Simone does not speak, cannot hold her head, move her arms or legs purposely, cannot sit up or stand, chokes on baby food, needs a feeding tube for all liquids and may not see well. But she will be 2 years old August 16th and she is greatly loved by all of her family and if all she can do is smile and sign, we are happy with that and we will carry on even though we will never know the what, the how or the why until the day we are told by God our father in heaven.

God bless and keep you and all those in your ministry.

Thank you sincerely,

Sharol

Prayer of Commitment

Father, these are good words for us, where our minds and hearts are renewed by Your Word and receive them. It's all true. As Your children we need to guard our behavior in the midst of trials. God, help us. We need to grace our relationships. Most of all, Lord, we want to bring glory to You. We want people to see the reality of who You are. It's all that will matter to us a hundred years from today. So give us that focus—not on the past, not on the future. **"Sufficient for the day are the cares of today"** *(Matthew 6:34).*

*And we entrust ourselves to You, faithful Creator. Give us strength to keep
doing good. Amen.*

FROM GOD'S HEART TO MINE:

1 Peter 4:7–10

The end of all things is at hand; therefore be self-controlled and sober-
minded for the sake of your prayers. Above all, keep loving one another
earnestly, since love covers a multitude of sins. Show hospitality to one another without grumbling. As each has received a gift, use it to serve one another, as good stewards of God's varied grace.

1 Peter 4:19

Therefore let those who suffer according to God's will entrust their souls
to a faithful Creator while doing good.

MINING FOR GOLD

1. Pause before you study and use the prayer at the end of the chapter to track the way your trials are clarifying your relationship with God.

2. Since the timing of trials is in God's hands, our attention must be on the immediate challenge. Which of the areas of action need special attention during your current trial: guard your behavior, grace your relationships, give away your gift, or glorify God?

3. For each of the areas of action listed above, identify the opportunities you have to make today a well-spent day during your trial.

4. Review the four specific suggested "first responses" when trials come upon you found in 1 Peter 4:12–19. They are: rejoice, don't be ashamed, do a self-exam, and entrust your soul to your faithful Creator. How well have you been practicing these?

5. Why is shame such a problem for believers when it comes to trials? What is it about God's use of trials and His love for you that can prevent shame from taking root?

But he knows the way that I take;

*when **he** has tried me, I shall come out as gold. Job 23:10*

God Initiates

His purpose is at the center of this trial.

Y ou can't get around it. Job 23:10 says, **"When *he* has tried me."** The "he" is God Himself. Have you ever wondered, Where did this trial come from? Who did this to me? Answer: God did. God allowed this to come into your life. He is the One who chose it. He could have prevented it. Sometimes He does; but often He does not.

Does God's involvement in your pain blow your mind? Beyond that, I hope that thought takes you to the place where you can trash the incorrect views of God that hurt and hinder your growth. We think God is supposed to be a certain way, like He's some cosmic dispensing machine. But when we pull the lever and what we want to happen doesn't happen, we get mad at God. The problem is, that's not who God is. God isn't passive—just waiting around for you to make choices. He creates the crises.

God is far more interested in your holiness than in your temporary happiness. God's love is a perfecting love, not a pampering love. He is the One holding the hammer and the chisel. He alone is the answer to the trial that you're facing. Next time you wonder what God could be up to, just say to yourself, "He's changing me," and you will be right. Try to imagine God Himself holding the hammer and chisel, sculpting your character into a likeness of Christ. God wants to demonstrate His power and splendor through your life. He wants to get you to the place where no matter what happens to you or what you go through, you trust Him and live to please Him. God won't stop until you are committed wholly to what He's doing in you and in the world.

Therefore lift your drooping hands and strengthen your weak knees, and make straight paths for your feet, so that what is lame may not be put out of joint but rather be healed. Strive for peace with everyone, and for the holiness without which no one will see the Lord. See to it that no one fails to obtain the grace of God; that no "root of bitterness" springs up and causes trouble, and by it many become defiled; that no one is sexually immoral or unholy like Esau, who sold his birthright for a single meal. For you know that afterward, when he desired to inherit the blessing, he was rejected, for he found no chance to repent, though he sought it with tears.

HEBREWS 12:12–17

CHAPTER 4

WHAT IF I REFUSE THIS

TRIAL?

In a previous book, *Gripped by the Greatness of God*, I shared the amazing story of how we were given a $53-million property in Elgin, Illinois. The facility consisted of eighty-five wooded acres with a 285,000-square-foot corporate office building and an enclosed nine-hundred-car parking garage. The title was turned over to the church by the Hobby Lobby company for the sum of one dollar.

I confess that there have been many days in the last few years when I would have gladly given the entire property back—and not even asked for the dollar. We got that property at the height of a growth spurt in our Rolling Meadows facility, where we were running multiple services and shuttle buses. This was back before the idea or technology for multiple campuses with teaching via satellite broadcasts had been perfected. So we were operating on the understanding that we would construct a large worship facility attached to the buildings we had been given in Elgin.

We approved plans and then raised money for the building. Construction was well under way when the first blip of trouble appeared on the screen in the form of an added expense of 2.3 million dollars' worth of piles that had to be driven into the ground to help support the weight of the building. This complication was discovered after we had already ordered the steel for the frame and roof of the building. The timing and cost of this glitch had a sizeable impact on the budget of the project.

"Life is 10 percent what happens to you, and 90 percent how you choose to deal with it."
—LOU HOLTZ,
HALL OF FAME COLLEGE FOOTBALL COACH

About this time I had an experience I probably could have considered ominous. I was driving to the building site and found myself behind one of the huge trucks that were delivering the steel columns and beams that would create the skeleton of the church. At the driveway to the church property, the truck driver discovered that he had slightly overshot the turn, so he backed up. He didn't see me. At first I didn't notice what he was doing because I was talking to my brother on the phone. The massive I-beam stuck out behind his trailer and the red flag hanging from the end finally warned me that the distance between me and it was closing in an alarming way. I looked back and found someone was right behind me—nowhere or way to back up. The next thing I knew, the beam sliced through my front windshield and stopped about where my head would have been if I hadn't ducked.

The truck stopped. The driver leaped from the cab, mortified by the sight of my skewered car. When he found out I was the pastor of the church to which he was delivering, he began to weep with distress. My car was pretty messed up, but I was fine.

After the expense of the unexpected piles, there came a second major complication: Some of the steel in the framework had twisted and contorted as it was being raised. Work had stopped. We were stuck with a defective steel skeleton standing uselessly in the sun.

Almost immediately, the blame game launched in earnest. The steel manufacturer was facing off against the steel erector. Other contractors were drawn into the fray and lawsuits began to appear from every direction. The entire project was shut down for seven months while the mess was agonizingly sorted out. As recounted in the introduction, millions of dollars of liens fell on the stalled project, and the church was in real danger of going bankrupt. We had already invested millions and were on the hook for millions more. The weight drove me to my face before God, utterly helpless.

A CRISIS CALL TO THE PRESIDENT

It all came down to a Thursday when it was clear to me that we were right on the brink. If something didn't change radically, we were going to lose everything. I called the president of the company that owned the company that had manufactured the steel. I got this man on the phone and I said, "I'm a Christian and the pastor of a church. I realize you don't know me, but here's my story." At the point I made the call, his company was holding $2.5 million dollars' worth of steel they were scheduled to send to us but had stopped shipment pending all the litigation. Meanwhile, we had spent an extra $2.5 million repairing and correcting their fabrication mistakes. We were out 2.5 million in fixes and they still owed us 2.5 million in steel.

Faced with legal gridlock and a rapidly decaying financial situation, I had little choice but to go around the lawyers and talk to someone at the top. After I made sure he knew the situation, I said to him, "I am about to lose everything I have worked on for the past twenty years if you cannot respond with some sense of reasonableness. Your company made this steel wrong. That's not a refutable point. If we have to go to court, that error will be proven." He knew the situation.

Just in case I reached him, I had gotten approval from the church leadership for a last-ditch effort to break the stalemate. The elders had given their blessing while shaking their heads and saying, "James, he'll never go for what you are proposing." But I could not see any other choice.

I continued with the president. "Sir, I'm going to make you a one-time offer right now. I'm going to give you until five o'clock tomorrow afternoon, Friday, to ship me the rest of the steel for free. If you do that, the value of the shipment will cover the cost we have already spent fixing your steel. We will not sue you for lost time or for damages or for any other costs associated with the original mistakes. We will sign a document absolving you from any further responsibility in these matters. But we will not pay you another cent."

As things stood at that moment, despite their obvious mistakes, they had levied liens against us for millions of dollars. I insisted those liens would have to be canceled. The arrival of the steel would close the book on our relationship. Before I finished, I told him, "Please understand that I take my word seriously. . . . I don't have a 'B' plan. But if you decide not to take me up on this offer, and deliver that steel for free, then I will tell you right now that I will lose this church and shift my entire focus on pursuing you. I will . . . have a mission—to get justice from your company. They will pay for their irresponsibility and their lack of integrity in all of this."

When I hung up the phone, all I could hear were the voices of good friends telling me that someone in that man's position would not agree to my proposal. I had a sleepless night, filled with a new understanding of prayer without ceasing. I now knew exactly how Nehemiah felt when he ended his prayer, **"O Lord, let your ear be attentive to the prayer of your servant, and to the prayer of your servants who delight to fear your name, and give success to your servant today, and grant him mercy in the sight of this man"** (Nehemiah 1:11). I had no doubt that if this plan succeeded, it would be evidence of God's mercy!

Friday morning started out with a silent phone. It remained silent as the day dragged on. At five minutes before five o'clock, he returned my call. He had set things in motion to ship the steel. The gridlock had been broken, the liens had been removed, and our future was preserved.

During many of those dark days with that steel structure looming over my life, I understood the temptation of refusing and rejecting the trial. But I couldn't get past the truth that God allows difficult circumstances to come in to our lives—some painful. Something painful intended to transform our conduct and our character.

Wouldn't it be great if we all responded quickly and submissively? But that acceptance is a hard place to get to, sometimes. The bottom line is you've got to accept it.

Well, what if I don't?

Yes, that's a sober and honest question. How loving of God to put a warning in Hebrews 12 that pictures the downward spiral of what happens when we refuse the trial He has allowed.

TRIALS CAN LEAD TO DISCOURAGEMENT

The first hazard sign you'll meet when you go through something difficult is discouragement. And that's why you see in Hebrews 12:12, **"Therefore lift your drooping hands and strengthen your weak knees."** The first time we heard this expression of "drooping hands and weak knees" was during the Israelites' desert journey to the Promised Land in Exodus 14:12. Try to imagine someone coming your way with drooping hands and weak knees. They might as well be wearing a sign across their chest: "Discouraged." Drooping hands and weak knees are the physical manifestations of a person whose life has become very hard.

"Make straight paths for your feet" (v.12). You know it's true. When you're going through a trial, you don't have any time or energy for a walk in the park. I want to get as fast as I can from Point A to Point B. I want everything simple, down to a science, because I don't have a lot of surplus energy when I'm going through a trial. Yet discouragement tends to result in wandering off the straight pathway. Clearly this command speaks to someone discouraged, yet willing to remain under God's hand, saying, "I want to learn this, God!" Trials don't exempt us from having to press forward, step by step, meeting God who is moving toward us.

If you know me at all, you know I have a special love for pastors. So you know when we got this SOS e-mail from a discouraged pastor's wife that my heart felt burdened immediately. She wrote,

> Dear Walk in the Word Ministries,
>
> I have been blessed by your ministry on AM 570 WMCA in NYC. My husband is a pastor here in Queens, NY. We are walking through some very difficult times here—a lot of spiritual battles. I am writing to plead with you to pray for us and specifically my husband.
>
> We are feeling overwhelmed by the responsibilities of ministry, and overwhelmed by the spiritual battles our church is facing at this time. We are threatening to buckle under the pressure of the war. We feel confused and overwhelmed. We are grieved, burdened, and burned. We lack the fullness of God as the intensity of ministry and all has sucked the life out of us.
>
> Please pray for us and our church—that we would allow the Lord to lead and, that we would trust Him, that He would restore us and lead us in paths of righteousness for His name's sake. Thank you.

I don't know how this story will end, but I know that grace is going to flow to that couple, that pastor, and that church, as they trust the Lord, even when their hearts are broken and they are discouraged. They are remaining under the pressure and God will meet them there with sustaining grace.

But what about the person who doesn't want to learn it? The one who cuts and runs?

What about the person who is in denial? Are you in denial? Maybe you're like . . .

Yeah, that's not my trial. God's not trying to teach me anything.

This isn't really happening.

We don't have a problem in our marriage.

I'm not facing any financial difficulty.

I'm not going to the doctor for tests. I'm going to be fine!

Denial heightens discouragement because we can't be in partnership with God over something that we're not really acknowledging or accepting.

Maybe you're into finger-pointing. "Oh yeah, there's a problem. I don't deny it. And the problem is you!" That's only going to heighten your discouragement.

Maybe blame-shifting is your avoidance strategy. "Oh yeah, there is a problem. And fine, the problem's me. But it's not my fault. It's because of all of you people! Everyone's driving me crazy!"

These faulty attitudes only heighten discouragement in your life because you're not embracing what God has allowed. You're not acknowledging that it's for your good.

The truth is, trials don't have to lead to discouragement that lasts. After any difficult season, there is going to be some grief. But the discouragement does not have to linger. You can heal. You can get up. You can go on in God's strength.

But if you don't, that discouragement is going to cause a more serious injury.

DISCOURAGEMENT LEADS TO DISLOCATION

Discouragement is a problem. But dislocation—that's serious business.

"Make straight paths for your feet, **so that what is lame may not be put out of joint but rather be healed**" (v. 13). The Holy Spirit describes one of God's children who is experiencing God's discipline as *lame*. God is turning on the pressure. When it's over, you're going to have a limp. Problem comes in if you try to get out from under the pressure when it's still on and that angle creates an injury. If you're not willing to submit to God and you resist and rebel and refuse His discipline, you're gonna get hurt.

It is pressure combined with the wrong angle that creates the injury. When you're playing basketball and you go up for a rebound, if you come down and don't get your feet back under you or you land on someone else's foot, you're going down. All of your weight comes crashing down on the wrong side of your ankle and you go right to the floor. If you're submitting to God and that pressure's coming down on you, He will give you the strength to bear up under much more. But if you refuse to remain under it, that angle creates crazy pain.

Hebrews 12:13 calls it "out of joint." The NIV translates that "disabled." The NKJV translates it well: "dislocated." It's one thing to have a sprained ankle; it's another thing to have a dislocated ankle. One of my basketball buddies is in a special category of athlete. He could get serious vertical action. One game he jumped so high that he hit his head on the rim and practically knocked himself out. Another time he jumped up at a wrong angle and came down hard on his elbow. It looked so gross to see his elbow dislocated—completely out of the joint. They say that a hip dislocation is the most painful thing a person can experience. It can only happen in a car accident or maybe in a strange football injury.

> MOST CHRISTIANS TREAT GOD'S DESIRE TO GET HOLINESS INTO THEIR LIVES LIKE HE'S GIVING THEM COD LIVER OIL.

A dislocation is very serious. God's Word says that His goal in this trial is to *heal* what is lame. God doesn't want this trial to devastate your life. He wants it to cause just enough pain to get your attention and so you learn the lesson: Let's get healed and go on to be the person God wants us to be. You resist now and a more serious injury is coming . . . and it'll last longer.

I'm telling you, it doesn't have to be this way.

"Strive for peace" (v. 14). Peace is the absence of relational strife. It could really be translated, "Strive for no strife." **"With everyone"** (v. 14). Some of you are like, "I'm *totally* getting along great with everybody at my house." Yeah? How about everybody in your neighborhood? How about everybody at church? Not just your favorite people, but everyone. And then notice: **"And for the holiness without which no one will see the Lord"** (v. 14). As a teacher of God's Word, when I tell people "Go for holiness," some make the craziest faces. Like they just smelled something bad. You know why? Because they don't have a clue about what holiness is. If they had more of it, they'd know how awesome it is. Sadly, most Christians treat God's desire to get holiness into their lives like He's giving them cod liver oil.

But holiness is fantastic. It's you operating according to the Manufacturer's specifications. Holiness is where you once and for all put behind yourself all the silly, surface, posing and posturing. You discard the attitude, *Look at me, aren't I a good boy?* And, *What do people think about me?*

Holiness is when you get over all that and get into the soul satisfying, saturating presence of God in your life. It was the air you were created to breathe! When you get that flowing in your life in increasing measure, any time the preacher mentions holiness, you will ask, *How do I get more of that?*! We've got to develop a whole different reaction than what we typically have when we hear the word *holiness.*

Without holiness, "no one will see the Lord," verse 14 says. "But I thought all I've got to do is turn from my sin and embrace Jesus Christ by faith and be forgiven, and I'll go to heaven." Yes, that's how you get on the salvation boat. But everybody who's really on the boat is fired up about holiness. Not always perfectly, but increasingly. They're fired up about holiness because if you get more, you want more! That's what holiness is really like. That's what James 2:20 means when it says, **"Faith without works is dead"** (NKJV). Not that works save you, but the people who have the saving faith perform good works. If your faith hasn't changed you, it hasn't saved you.

So the real saving faith results in works, fruit, and a desire for holiness. The Bible's very consistent. It's all the same message; it just uses different terms.

In your trial, God is going for more holiness in you.

Trials can lead to discouragement.

Discouragement leads to dislocation.

Unless you turn around, this next step continues in severity.

So if you get the serious injury, and you still don't accept the trial, and you still don't allow yourself to be trained by it and you don't say, "God, as painful as this is—I know it's from You and I'm going to get the good out of it," you're going in the wrong direction fast.

"See to it that no one fails to obtain the grace of God" (v. 15). This is one of the more important phrases dealing with trials. If you know someone who's going through a trial, make sure they don't "fail to obtain the grace of God." See to it. If you're married, make sure that your husband or wife doesn't fail to obtain the grace of God.

Make sure that your pastor doesn't fail to obtain the grace of God.

Make sure that your brother doesn't fail to obtain the grace of God.

Let's all take care of each other.

WHAT IS A PERSON DOING IN A TRIAL IF THEY'RE NOT GETTING GOD'S GRACE? THEY COULD BE WHITE-KNUCKLING IT.

What does that mean—to fail "to obtain the grace of God"? Galatians 5:4 explains, **"You have become estranged from Christ, you who attempt to be justified by law; you have fallen from grace"** (NKJV). You failed to obtain the grace. Falling short of the grace in salvation is you trying to save you. Falling short of the grace in sanctification is trying to sanctify yourself—to make yourself holy. So God puts a trial in your life and instead of submitting to the trial, agreeing *God, You're in charge.*

Jesus, You're Lord—I'm not! you resist and rebel and refuse the trial. You fight against it.

Now you're failing to obtain the grace of God. Don't let that happen to anyone *you* know.

What is a person doing in a trial if they're not getting God's grace? They're faking it. They could be white-knuckling it. That's where you pretend (*Hang on, man! We're going to get through this!*), just trying to gut it out. But you're not walking with God. You're not digging into His Word. You're not kneeling down and praying. You're not turning up the volume of all the spiritual dials in your soul. You're just getting through it. You're also not getting the grace of God. It's not going anywhere good.

Or you could be putting on the hyper-submission act. We've talked about this before. *Go ahead, God! Just run me over! Where's the steamroller? Start it up! Bring it now! Do it again!* Trials do not accomplish their beneficial work when we respond with a victim mentality.

These responses might sound spiritual but you're not partnering with God. You're either doing it on your own or you're hyper-submissive. Both of those extremes are what God's Word is talking about here.

DISLOCATION CAN LEAD TO BITTERNESS.

How can I know if I'm responding the wrong way? Verse 15 tells us. **"See to it that no one fails to obtain the grace of God; that no 'root of bitterness' springs up and causes trouble, and by it many become defiled."**

Deuteronomy 29:18 warns us, **"Beware lest there be among you a root bearing poisonous and bitter fruit."** Moses is not talking about a plant; he's talking about a poisonous person. Here is the profile of a bitter person: **"One who, when he hears the words of this sworn covenant, blesses himself in his heart, saying, 'I shall be safe, though I walk in the stubbornness of my heart'"** (v. 19).

That's the bitter person. The trial comes, but I don't want it. I say to myself, *I will be safe, though I walk in the stubbornness of my heart. I hear what the Word of God says. It's taught to me. I understand it, but I go on with life because I think,* I will be safe, though I walk in the stubbornness of my heart. I don't care what you say. *I don't care what the Bible says. I'm* never *going to be happy about this thing that's happened to me! Don't you ever ask to try to find a place of joy about this! I'm not happy about it!*

Those thinking patterns reveal what you are: You're bitter. *I'm not going to let God change me.* You should. He wants to. We all want Him to.

This will help: Everyone is so ready for you to change. What's more bitter than living with a bitter person? God's Word describes your condition as a **"root of bitterness"** (Hebrews 12:15). It gets in and swirls and snarls its way around your soul. It clouds your judgment. It distorts the way you see everything. It doesn't have to be that way. I know people who have been through the darkest, most unimaginable series of valleys. Not just one thing, but three, four, or five tragedies that shouldn't happen to one person. Instead of feeling bitter, they have the sweetest, most precious heart for the Lord, and it comes out in everything that they do.

> A ROOT OF BITTERNESS. . . SNARLS ITS WAY AROUND YOUR SOUL. IT CLOUDS YOUR JUDGMENT.

I know other people who have been through a lot less and are so cold, calloused, and twisted. They have a root of bitterness. Here's the bad news: You think the root's ugly? Wait until you see the tree. Notice that it says there that a "root of bitterness **springs up**." It's coming out! Your attitude toward the trial that God has allowed might be a secret for a while, but it's not going to be a secret forever. Eventually it's coming out. When that bitterness comes out, it **"causes trouble, and by it many become defiled"** (v. 15). "Defiled" is the word translated "torment" in Luke 6:18. It's what demons do to people. It is an *extremely* destructive thing to have in your heart.

"Dude, where did this ugly tree come from?"

I *told* you. God has allowed a trial to come into your life, and you are refusing it. Perhaps God has not allowed you to have children or you can't find a career you want or you've experienced a profound loss or a life-changing injury or illness. Instead of accepting that this is what God in His wisdom has chosen for you, that He's appointed to you a season of adversity, you're like, *I don't want it! I refuse it! I deeply resent it!* Discouragement becomes dislocation. You're trying to get out from under it; the angle causes the injury. Now it's getting worse but instead of getting humble, you get bitter.

And the bitterness is defiling many people. Bitterness cannot be tolerated in a home or it will ruin a marriage and it will ruin the children. Bitterness cannot be tolerated in a church or it will ruin the love and the joy that's there. It's a difficult thing as an elder in a church to have to move toward someone and deal with bitterness. Make sure you give the leaders of your church room to deal with bitter people. Confronting bitterness is always a very messy process.

But you still have a way out. God promised an escape route to temptation and here's yours: Get a deep, heartfelt repentance and submission to God going on your part. Because if you don't:

Trials lead to discouragement.

Discouragement leads to dislocation.

Dislocation leads to bitterness.

And finally . . .

BITTERNESS LEADS TO PROFANE LIVING

Profane living means godlessness. Verse 15 begins, **"See to it that no one fails."** Verse 16, continuing the same thought expands, **"that no one is sexually immoral or unholy like Esau."** Do you remember Esau? After the no-sin thing didn't work with Adam and Eve and the fresh start didn't work with Noah, God said, "I'll choose a nation." So He set Abraham apart. Abraham had a son named Isaac, and Isaac and Rebecca had twins boys: Esau and Jacob.

While many translations use the term "sexually immoral" (including ESV, NIV), and others use "fornicator" (including NKJV), some simply say "immoral" (NASB) to refer to Esau's reputation. But the Old Testament account (Genesis 25–36) does not specifically describe Esau as sexually immoral or a fornicator. The context here in Hebrews helps us see what the writer had in mind. The Bible consistently indicates that the greatest form of sin is not unfaithfulness to your partner or unfaithfulness to your own body—but unfaithfulness to God. Look at these references:

You have played the whore with many lovers; and would you return to me?" declares the Lord. (Jeremiah 3:1)

You adulterous people! Do you know that friendship with the world is enmity with God? (James 4:4)

So the greatest form of unfaithfulness is unfaithfulness to God. And I think that's what Hebrews 12:16 is saying here. Esau was unfaithful to God. Spiritual issues meant nothing to Esau. That's why one translation here uses *unholy*; NIV and NASV say that he was *godless*. NKJV is a great translation, *profane*. It means the literal of which *fornicator* is the figurative; it means that Esau was unhallowed; the things of God meant nothing to Him. Jacob and Esau were twins, but Esau was born first. By birth order, Esau had the birthright and the blessing, which was God's favor tied up into those two things.

The twins could not have been more different. Jacob loved to stay at home with his mother, cooking and making food in the kitchen. Esau liked to hunt. Esau would be perfect on the cover of *Outdoorsman* magazine. But the big difference was that Jacob, in spite of his faults, loved God. And Esau, in spite of the way he was tricked, was never humble and broken; never in submission to God.

You remember the story: Esau comes in one day from hunting. Jacob is in the kitchen. You can read it yourself in Genesis 25. Esau was get-out-of-my-way-or-I'll-kill-you hungry. "Give me whatever you're making there," he demanded. Jacob, seeing his opportunity, said, in essence, "Yeah, that smells kind of good, doesn't it?" And then bargained, "Sell me your birthright for this bowl of soup."

Now what Esau should've said was, "Are you crazy? For my birthright, I could buy a river of stew!" But he was a profane person. The birthright was a spiritual thing. It was given in a blessing; a prayer from the father. The things of God didn't mean anything to Esau. All he could think of was his immediate discomfort.

So instead of valuing his heritage, Esau basically said, "Whatever! Who cares about the birthright. Give me my stew!"

So Jacob thought, *Sweet! That was easy!* And he served up the stew for his brother.

Now that is a tragic moment in Scripture. It shows the heart of a profane person demonstrating that God means nothing to him. Esau sold the birthright in a moment, but inwardly his disregard for the holy birthright had been around for a long time. As I often say, the crises of life are a way of revealing something that's been happening for a long time.

THE CRISES OF LIFE ARE A WAY OF REVEALING SOMETHING THAT'S BEEN HAPPENING FOR A LONG TIME.

We've all heard these horror stories. The ones that make us shake our heads and ask, "What would cause a faithful mother of fifteen years to turn her back on her husband and on her children and run off with some cheesy loser?" "What would cause a businessman who has decades of integrity under his belt to all of a sudden, in a moment, make some awful decision and lose everything just to thicken his wallet?" "What would cause a pastor who's preached God's Word faithfully for years to . . . "

A blowout doesn't happen in three minutes. Something has been going on below the surface for a long time. It may have started with discouragement, which was followed by dislocation, which grew into bitterness that eventually led to profane living. Inevitably, refusing the trial that God has let into your life will burst forth in profane living. It will. It's going to come out. You won't be able to keep it all down forever: All that anger and bitterness and resentment to God will eventually come out. And you may well verbalize your inner thoughts:

"Why do I have to go over to that church again?"

"I never touch my Bible from week to week. It doesn't mean anything to me."

You're angry inside. You resent what God's given to other people and you feel like you've been bypassed. That bitterness in you is going to come out. In some way . . . As private pornography? As secret lust? As a deep resentment?

If you don't get in a place of submission to God, **"be sure your sin will find you out,"** Numbers 32:23 says. It's all going to come out. Jesus wasn't kidding when He said, **"Therefore whatever you have said in the dark shall be heard in the light, and what you have whispered in private rooms shall be proclaimed on the housetops"** (Luke 12:3).

This is a warning message.

Bitterness leads to profane living. To further the agenda of refusing God, the persistent rebel inevitably goes to profane living like Esau did **"who sold his birthright for a single meal."**

I wish that was the end. I wish I could stop right now, but I have to tell you there's a final step in this downward spiral of refusing what God has allowed.

PROFANE LIVING LEADS TO DISQUALIFICATION

Eventually, if you continue down this path of refusing the Lord, what you're really doing is giving proof that you never really have known the Lord. That's why it says in Hebrews 12:17, **"For you know that afterward, when he desired to inherit the blessing, he was rejected, for he found no chance to repent, though he sought it with tears."**

This is one of the scariest verses in the entire Bible. A lot of Christians think, *I can do what I want. I can think what I want. I'll get right with God when I'm good and ready.* What a foolish line of thinking that is, like you can produce a genuine thirst for holiness whenever you want? That a right relationship with God is something that you create at will? He is a fool who thinks he can put off repentance until it is convenient.

Any step you've ever made spiritually has only been by the grace of God. And you can't refuse and resist and rebel against God's grace and then just clue in some day and change. *I can come back to God when I'm good and ready!* You should study the Bible more carefully. Genesis 6:3 (NKJV) says, **"My Spirit shall not strive with man forever."** There comes a time when God says, "You think that thing you need to have is so great? You think that's better than Me? Do you think that's going to satisfy you? Why don't you go and have that then?"

And God turns us over to the things that we think we have to have. That's what happened in Numbers 11:20 when Israel demanded meat. The Bible says that God gave it until it was running out of their nostrils, until they were choking on it. It's a sick picture. Referencing that same scene, the psalmist said in 106:15, **"[God] gave them their request, but sent leanness into their soul"** (NKJV).

Then, after you have what you thought you had to have, then you think you should really have God too. **"For you know that afterward"** (Hebrews 12:17). It's always afterward. After I have what I had to have, then I want God, too.

"I want my private pleasure . . . *and* God."

"I want my gluttonous pursuit . . . *and* God."

"I want my material objective . . . *and* God."

"I want *both!*" That's not going to happen.

Back to Esau's sad story. "For you know that afterward, **when he desired to inherit the blessing . . .**" (v. 17). Poor Esau woke up and realized, *What was I thinking? I gave up my birthright for stew? Now that I had what I wanted, now I'm going to go get what really matters!* Ah, bad plan.

Because look at this: "Afterward, when he desired to inherit the blessing, **he was rejected**" (v. 17). "Rejected." That's a word that is translated "reprobate" (KJV) and "disqualified" in Romans 1:28 and 1 Corinthians 9:27. It's a horrible term that Paul used to describe his own appropriate concern— **"lest after preaching to others, I myself should be disqualified."**

Paul? Paul was fearful of not making the grade? Right! Paul was aware that his assurance of salvation was not rooted in a prayer that he prayed. That's how you *get* saved. But Paul's assurance of salvation was tied up in,

"Does my life give evidence of a person who is saved?" The apostle thought, *The last thing I want to do is be a guy who's out there talking about it to other people, but I'm not living it.*

ALWAYS IN SCRIPTURE, THE TIME TO RESPOND TO GOD IS TODAY— NOW.

I feel that. The last thing I can afford to do is tell you all about trials, and not live it in my own life. But you can be encouraged that I *am* going through it and that I *am* seeking to submit fully and to embrace what God has allowed in my life. That's what you need to do, too. There will come a time when there's no more time. In the meantime, people are watching your life who will never know me. You are the one who can be a living example of submission to God.

How do I know if it's too late for me? Well, if you care, it's not too late. But if you've stumbled upon this page and you are like, *What is he talking about? Blah, blah, blah*—that attitude should scare you. You should suspect a root of bitterness growing within you. You may have expressed profanity in thought or action.

Psalm 95:7 says, **"Today, if you hear his voice, do not harden your heart."** *Why today?* Because you don't know if you're going to get tomorrow. You might not have another chance. You don't know if God is ever again going to stir tenderness in your heart that you might be feeling right now. Always in Scripture, the time to respond to God is today—now.

"For you know that afterward when he desired to inherit the blessing, he was rejected, **for he found no chance to repent**" (v. 17). He couldn't repent **"though he sought it with tears."** The NIV inserts the phrase "though he sought **the blessing** with tears." That's not in the original. Esau was not seeking *the blessing* with tears, he was seeking the place of repentance. He tried to repent and he couldn't. He couldn't be sorry about it, because his heart was too hard. He already had the stew. How do you eat the stew and consume it and then be sorry that you ate it? *The whole time your mind is*

*racing, You're not sorry! You already got what you wanted. You're just playing
a game with God.*

God doesn't play games. Repentance is a serious thing. Repentance is
actually changing your mind. It's not easy to repent.

Second Timothy 2:25 says that **"God may perhaps grant them repentance."** I know that there's repentance needed in your house as there is in
mine. Repentance is a good gift from God. We need to ask God to give us
repentance over the hard-hearted, bitter attitude with which we have responded to the difficult season He's allowed in our life. We need to come to
a place of genuine, true submission to God about what He's allowed.

I can recall a man in my church who was going through a very painful
season in his family. He was a new Christian, only a year or so in the Lord,
when a very loved family member unexpectedly died. The funeral was going
to be a seriously painful event because the person who died did not know
the Lord as their personal Savior. My friend was leaning hard on the Lord.

When the family gathered together, all his siblings and children, he got
up and went over to his stereo and put in the song our church sings in worship, *It's All About You.* And he just sat there, and asked his whole family to
listen. Then he said these very profound words for a young believer, "I want
God to know that I don't just love Him because I'm going to heaven someday, and I don't just love Him because He does what's good for me, I love
God no matter what!"

No matter what. *No matter what, I will trust You. No matter what, I will
believe You are working a plan that will be for Your glory and my good. No
matter what, I refuse to be bitter.* How hot can the furnace get and can you
still say, "No matter what, I love God, and I am committed to Him"?

Does God have you in the furnace right now? He's refining you like gold.
Grace will flow to the person who will say through their tears,

It's all about You, Jesus

And all this is for You

For Your glory and Your fame
It's not about me
As if You should do things my way
You alone are God and I surrender
To Your ways.

Jesus, lover of my soul
All consuming fire is in Your gaze
Jesus, I want You to know
I will follow You all my days.

For no one else in history is like You
And history itself belongs to You
Alpha and Omega, You have loved me
And I will spend eternity with You.

["Jesus, Lover of My Soul It's All About You." Written by Paul Oakley ©1995. Thankyou Music. International copyright secured. All rights reserved. Used by permission.]

Prayer of Commitment

God, it's not about me. It's not about my position or my pleasure. It's about You, God. I've been refusing this trial, God. I've been resisting it. I just want to ask for Your forgiveness. Oh God, would You grant to me an unusual submission to You? This is the life that You have marked out for me. My parents are who they are. My friends, my situation in life, my marital status, our children—all of it, God. Wherever I am, this is Your plan for me here and now. You're God and I am not, and I want to submit to You, God. Forgive my rebelliousness. Forgive my stubbornness, God. Forgive my walking in the strength of my own heart in thinking that I could be safe. Forgive me.

Draw my heart back to You, God. You say in Your Word " (James 4:8) that if I draw near to You, You will draw near to me. I don't want to fall short of the grace, God. I know I need it and I want it. I can't get through this on my own. So give to me Your grace and strength. Forgive my stubborn, rebellious ways. And draw me close to Yourself, God. Even as I draw near to You.

FROM GOD'S HEART TO MINE

1 John 3:1

See what kind of love the Father has given to us, that we should be called children of God.

Hebrews 3:15

Today, if you hear his voice, do not harden your heart.

MINING FOR GOLD

1. Pause before you study. Use the prayer at the end of the chapter to slow down and give God time to speak to you.

2. This chapter describes five stations spiraling downward when we refuse the benefits of trials: discouragement, dislocation, bitterness, profane living, and disqualification. At what point are you right now in responding to your trials?

3. Are you spiraling up or spiraling down? Why?

4. What is the first step required to turn a downward spiral into an upward one when it comes to responding to trials (see Psalm 95:7 and Hebrews 12:17)?

5. How do you respond to the statement in this chapter's Glimpse of Gold: "God is more interested in your holiness than in your temporary happiness"?

6. As a result of this chapter, have you found you are definitely refusing to accept one or more trials that God has allowed into your life? What is keeping you from repentance?

But he knows the way that I take;

*when he **has tried me**, I shall come out as gold.* Job 23:10

God Reveals

This trial will show me what I need.

The day is coming when the test will be over ... and I will have discovered something very important ... once God **has tried me.**

I remember working with my grandfather on his farm. All day in the hot sun would get the best of us and I'd aggravate him. He'd say, "You're starting to *try* my patience, boy!" Okay, now I get it. What he meant was that he didn't know how much patience he had and I was helping him find out. That was kind of good of me, as I look back.

That's sort of like what's going on today in your trial—the only difference is that God already knows how much you can take. The trial isn't for God to find out but for you to find out what you have and what you need to have in order to be who God wants you to be.

When you're feeling the pressure, the first thing you want to do is get out from under it. In your work, in your marriage, and in your walk with Christ, the temptation is persistent to cut and run. You want relief, but God wants maturity. You want release, but God wants you to remain under until the lesson is learned.

The test is on. God allows trials into your life to stretch your faith. Will you believe what He has said or will you bail? Will your responses reflect the superiority of a life lived in God? With great love and perfect wisdom, God is *trying* your faith. And after **he has tried** you, life won't return to normal; it will move up to better.

So to keep me from becoming conceited because of the surpassing greatness of the revelations, a thorn was given me in the flesh, a messenger of Satan to harass me, to keep me from being conceited. Three times I pleaded with the Lord about this, that it should leave me. But he said to me, "My grace is sufficient for you, for my power is made perfect in weakness." Therefore I will boast all the more gladly of my weaknesses, so that the power of Christ may rest upon me. For the sake of Christ, then, I am content with weaknesses, insults, hardships, persecutions, and calamities. For when I am weak, then I am strong.

2 CORINTHIANS 12:7–10

CHAPTER 5

WHY SOME TRIALS NEVER
END

Recently Kathy and I were wandering around some California hill country, enjoying one of our long walks together. I must have brushed up against some thistle, because I found these little pointy, sticky thorns in my leg. Later I touched them, and soon I had three or four stuck in my hand. Then, like a real brainiac, I tried to get one out with my teeth. Now I had one in my lip. I went to the mirror but though I couldn't even see it, I totally could feel it!

Multiply that kind of pain in intensity and you know what it's like to have a splinter in your soul. Only then are you ready to do absolutely whatever it takes to get relief.

UNDERSTANDING YOUR THORN

A thorn. The word *thorn* is used only once in the New Testament, in 2 Corinthians 12:7 (NASB): **"To keep me from exalting myself, there was given me a thorn in the flesh"** The Greek word literally means *a splinter; a* *stake; a thorn.* It's a small piece of wood imbedded in the skin that causes injury. And really—the pain is disproportionate to its size.

The apostle Paul is famous for his thorn. So what was it? A lot of ink has been spilled trying to answer that question. Tertullian, a church historian, said it was headaches. Ramsey said it was epilepsy. Luther said that it was demonic oppression. Augustine said that it was his relational adversaries in Corinth.

God knows much better than we do just how much we can actually take with His help.

I had a college professor who thought it was eye problems because in Galatians 6:11, Paul says, **"See with what large letters I am writing to you."** Paul was writing in big, block letters, so the guess is that he couldn't see very well.

Some people say it was a character flaw that vexed him. One commentator said it was hysteria. Another categorically said it was gallstones.

I thought this was also a good guess: Someone said it was hypochondria.

Someone else said it was a besetting sin.

A THORN IS AN ENDURING SOURCE OF PERSONAL PAIN ALLOWED BY GOD FOR YOUR GOOD.

Luther also thought that it was sexual temptation. Paul was single and living in Ephesus. Do the math on that one.

The fact is that we don't know. How about that?

The Bible doesn't tell us what the thorn was. If God wanted us to know, He would have told us. I think it's awesome that we don't know, because now you can think it's your thing; I think it's my thing; we all think it's the thing we suffer with. I'm just like Paul—I have a thorn. And that's not bad. That's not bad that we can all look into God's Word and find comfort like

Paul found and be strengthened and ministered to as Paul was. I think it's immensely wise of God's Spirit in the inspiration of Scripture not to disclose to us what the thorn was.

A thorn is enduring trial. Normal trials we get over with; they don't go on forever. Thorns stick around. James 1:12 makes it clear, **"Blessed is the man who remains steadfast under trial, for when he has stood the test . . ."**

1 Peter 4:12 tells us concerning **"the fiery trial [that] comes upon you to test you,"** it comes for a season and then it leaves. The fire goes out.

Hebrews 12:11 agrees that normal trials are just for a season, **"For the moment all discipline seems painful rather than pleasant, but later it yields the peaceful fruit of righteousness to those who have been trained by it."** So, eventually a normal trial gets done but the same is not true for a thorn. Not every Christian gets a thorn. A thorn is an enduring source of personal pain allowed by God for our good.

ALLOWED BY GOD

That phrase *allowed by God* needs some clarification. Honestly, it's a mystery. How could a loving God allow painful, difficult things to happen even as He does? This word *allowed* is really important. Not *directly caused*—not by God. Did God give me cancer? Some people whose faith and theology I greatly respect would say, *Yes, He did.* But I do not believe that.

Did God cause the tsunami that happened in Indonesia on the day after Christmas 2004? Did God part the earth and ripple the water that caused 300,000 people to be swept to their deaths? Did God cause the heartache and destruction that blew in with Hurricane Katrina? Some would say, "Yes, He did."

This is important for us to think through. When I walk through deep valleys with people in my church, we frame their trials within these five borders:

1. Omnipotence Has Its Limits.

When you say that God is all powerful, you have to know what you're talking about. Theologians used to wrestle with questions like: *Can God make a rock so big He can't lift it?* Ah, no, He cannot! Because no matter how big He made it He can lift it. But what if He made it twice as big as that? Be careful with the questions you form. Omnipotence doesn't mean that God can do absolutely anything that you can conceive of.

There are many things God can't do. God "cannot lie" (Titus 1:2 NASB). Nor can God make a round square. God cannot make a married bachelor, though some have tried. Either you're married or you're not.

But I thought God could do anything! God can do anything that can be done. Those other concepts are logical contradictions. God can't contradict nor contra-act Himself. Now file that away for a moment and we'll come back to it.

2. The World That God Made Is Good.

In its original form, as God designed and instituted it, this world was perfect. But it was a very particular kind of world that God chose to make—He wanted to make a world in which people were free to choose. He could have made a world where we were all robots. He could have made a world where we all came over to the church on Sunday morning at 11:00 a.m. and said, "I worship You. Amen." He could've made it so we all did that *perfectly*—every time! But how much would that mean to Him?

If I said to my wife, "Honey, it's Sunday morning at 11:00 a.m. It's time to tell you I love you again. So, 'I love you.' I'll see you next week"—how meaningful would that be? Not very. My wife doesn't want that and neither does God. He doesn't want robotic worship. God wants meaningful worship. In order to have meaningful worship, God had to create us with the opportunity to choose. In order to have meaningful obedience, there had to be the possibility of volitional disobedience.

3. God Made a World in Which People Are Truly Free to Choose.

People are free to choose, which means not everyone will choose Him. God prefers the meaningful worship of the few over the robotic worship of the masses. He took a pass on a puppet creation. Because He chose to make a world in which people were free to choose, He could not make a world in which people were free to choose *and*, at the same time, guarantee that everyone would choose Him.

4. The Effects of Sin Visit Themselves Randomly upon the Creation.

Given the kind of world that God wanted to create, the effects of sin visit themselves randomly upon the creation. In a world in which man and woman were free to choose, we chose to sin. And because Adam and Eve chose sin, the creation is broken (Genesis 3:17, 18; Romans 8:20). The world doesn't work right. People get cancer. People die prematurely. Accidents happen. People get sick. I'm not saying that we're not responsible for that; I'm just saying that the whole thing is broken.

5. God Could Prevent the Effects of Sin.

Remember, God made a world in which people are free to choose (border 3 above). God could not make a world with freedom of choice and at the same time guarantee everyone would choose Him. When people do not choose God, they bring consequences upon themselves and everyone else.

I believe that occasionally God does intervene, but normally God allows the broken creation to go on as it is and for horrible events to happen. God allows those things. Then this is what He does instead: He inserts Himself post-event and promises Himself to the people who are facing the trial so that we can display the superiority of the life lived in God. We go through the same things that people who don't know the Lord go through and yet our experience is so different.

DOES GOD CAUSE CALAMITY?

But James, there are some pictures in Scripture that show God more than causally involved—not just allowing, but causing. Yes, some Scripture does indicate that.

Isaiah 45:7 says, **"I make well-being and create calamity, I am the Lord, who does all these things."** Yes, He does create calamity ultimately in that He chose to create a world in which people were free to choose. In that sense, God is involved in it.

Jonah 1:4, 17 says that **"The Lord hurled a great wind up on the sea"** and **"the Lord appointed a fish."** God didn't make the fish or the storm out of nothing and put it right in front of Jonah. God guided the natural order of events to accomplish His purposes. But there's a serious problem if you make God causally related to the things that happen in the world because of sin.

God's relationship to cause is this: He created a good world in which people were free to choose. And because mankind has chosen sin, we live in a broken world. But our God is not the god of deism, who created the world and then let it spin out of control while He went off to do something else. Our God, who revealed Himself through creation, His Word, and His Son, is intimately aware and involved in our lives. God sometimes intervenes, but most often He allows and uses events in this broken world for our good.

SATAN'S GOAL IN OUR PAIN

So back to 2 Corinthians 12 and our original question. *Who is the source of Paul's thorn?* Many people think *God gave it to him.* But if you look at the text, that's really not what it says. Notice: **"So to keep me from being conceited because of the surpassing greatness of the revelations, a thorn was given me in the flesh, a messenger of Satan"** (v. 7).

The apostle Peter is the target of a lot of jokes. He comes across as an awkward, clumsy guy who didn't know much except fishing. He was so transparently flawed that we find it easy to see our own flaws in him. He was weak when he denied Christ; he was impulsive in spite of the great strength that he showed in Matthew 16 confessing Jesus Christ as Lord. He alone joined Jesus for a stroll on the water, but then went under when he saw the waves. But it's interesting, in Luke 22:31 (NKJV), Jesus said to him, **"Simon, Satan has asked for you, that he may sift you as wheat."**

Now, did God cause that? No, He did not. But just like in the case of Job, just like in the case of so many of us, God allowed that. God permitted Peter's suffering within boundaries. And God permitted Paul's thorn. God remained sovereign and was intimately aware of events without directly intervening.

Notice that phrase, "messenger of Satan." Allowed by God, sent by Satan. Satan was the messenger of Paul's thorn. Many Scriptures point to Satan or one of his demons as the deliverer of suffering.

In Matthew 9:33, a demon caused a man to be mute.

In Matthew 12:22, a demon caused a man to be blind and mute.

In Matthew 17:15, a demon caused a man to have seizures.

In Luke 13:16, Satan caused a woman to be bent over. Look it up yourself. For eighteen years Satan kept her in that position. It was a thorn allowed by God sent by Satan.

> SATAN'S GOAL IS TO PARALYZE YOU WITH FEAR . . . TO MAKE YOU THINK ALL IS LOST AND NOTHING WILL CHANGE.

"A messenger of Satan to harass me" (v. 7). The NASB and NIV say, **"to torment me."** The NKJV says **"to buffet me."** Literally the term means "to strike with the fist; to box; or to punch." It's a strong word. The immediate results are bumps and bruises; painful, but not fatal. In Matthew 26:57 when a high priest allowed them to strike Jesus, this is the exact same phrase for the blows inflicted on Jesus, translated here when Paul says, **"A messenger of Satan to torment me** (NASB). It's a very strong term.

Satan's goal is to harass and torment us. His goal is to paralyze you with fear; to pummel you into painful hopelessness; to make you think all is lost and nothing will change. That's your thorn. Whatever form it takes, that's its purpose. Thorns are real. They are lasting, tormenting, and below it all, satanic. Paul says it's "a thorn in my flesh" but that doesn't mean it's only physical.

Maybe it's in my mind; a persistent doubt.

Maybe it's in my emotions; a grief that won't fade.

Maybe it's in my will; a stubborn, persistent point of failure.

GOD CAN TURN THE THORN TO OUR GOOD

Satan's goal is to harass and torment you.

But if God's goal wasn't to use the thorn for your good, He would not have allowed it. You need to be sure of that. He has promised that He **"causes all things to work together for good to those who love God"** (Romans 8:28 NASB). You don't have to be able to see it; you don't have to be able to conceive of it; it's not up to you to have a plan to figure it out. That's not on you! That is on God to figure that out. You may never be able to figure it out, but He has promised and it's His goal to use it for good.

Through Humbling Us

"To keep me from being conceited" (v. 7) is how Paul describes the positive effects of the thorn. The NASB translates this, **"To keep me from exalting myself."** Something here is on the line. Now you might think, *Paul's problem may have been pride, but that's certainly not my problem.* Careful. More than ego or an inflated sense of self-importance, a much more insidious pride could be your sense of independence.

I can handle this. I can fix this. I can settle this.

That's where the thorn's going—to keep me from coming to the place in my life where I think *I have it going on! There's really not a whole lot that could tank my boat. I've learned how to navigate through life. Nothing can really make me go under at this point.* That's the pride factor he's going for.

He's applying his own words from 1 Corinthians 10:12, **"Therefore let anyone who thinks that he stands take heed lest he fall."**

I talked to a man on the phone today who I've known and loved for years. I could barely hear his voice through his weeping. He's learning this. This is what he said:

"Today's the best day of my life." He could hardly talk. Through his sobs, he said, "I finally see it. I can't do this myself. I'm not smart enough. I'm not dedicated enough. I'm not even godly enough." Only as he stared with stark finality down the throat of his total inability to accomplish what was in front of him did he come to the place where he could say, "I get it. It's not about me."

Through Humbling Me

I have a favorite story that bears repeating. Several years ago I was greeting people after the service down in front of the church when a woman I didn't know approached me. She was clearly upset. She wanted to tell me something that one of my staff had said—something I'm sure he didn't say, and certainly something I don't have ears to hear about the men with whom I labor shoulder to shoulder. All that to say, I tried to help, I couldn't, and she didn't listen very well. It was a very painful conversation.

I had another pastor pray with her and I thought that was the end of it until later that week, when I received a very hurtful letter from her. After rehearsing the situation from her perspective, she closed with, "You're nothing but a donkey—a big donkey."

That just wasn't a great day and, I've got to admit I was pretty upset about it. Normally I would have dismissed it but I was overtired and dealing with other hard issues. For two days I walked around thinking, *I'm nothing but a donkey—a big donkey.* It just got lodged in my spirit and I couldn't get rid of it.

I had received that poisonous letter on Wednesday. On Friday, I was having lunch with the pastor of Chicago's Moody Church, Erwin Lutzer. He's been a mentor to me and I really respect him. So we chatted over lunch, but I didn't tell him anything about the donkey comment because I didn't have it figured out myself.

At the end of our lunch, Dr. Lutzer walked me back to my car and he said, "You know, James, God is really using your life."

I said, "Thanks." It meant a lot to me for him to say that.

Then he said, "So you need to stay humble." *Well, that's a good word. Who doesn't need to hear that?* And I thanked him for that.

And then he looked at me and right out of the blue he said, " . . . Because you know what they say about the donkey, don't you?" For real he said that.

I was just like, "Uh, no. What do they say?"

He said, "Even the donkey knew that the palm branches and the blankets were for the Person on his back and not for him."

Well, I got out of there fast—into my car and on the freeway. I'm not embarrassed to tell you that I shed a few tears on the way home as I had this great time with the Lord. *That is it! I am a donkey! It doesn't matter about me. It doesn't matter what people say. It doesn't matter what people think about me. Because it's not about me! It's about You, Lord! Everything I do— it's for You! I have to keep reminding myself. Even a donkey knows that!*

You cannot tell me that God did not put that word on Pastor Lutzer's heart to say to me and I received it as a word from the Lord!

ACCEPTING THE THORN

Don't ever think you know why someone else is going through something. But whatever God's reasons are, when He wants to get that lesson through—it's thorn time. Right then.

You're going to "get" this.

But Lord, I think I already have it.

You're going to "get it" like you've never had it before. That thorn will hurt in a place you haven't hurt before. It's going to hurt longer than it's ever hurt before. But you're going to be changed by it.

Why was God doing this to Paul? Look at verse 1.

Paul's spiritual résumé was awesome. But the Corinthians were questioning him constantly: attacking his apostleship, his motives, his speaking style, everything. In 2 Corinthians 12:1, Paul was defending his apostleship:

> **I must go on boasting. Though there is nothing to be gained by it, I will go on to visions and revelations of the Lord. I know a man in Christ who fourteen years ago was caught up to the third heaven—whether in the body or out of the body I do not know, God knows. And I know that this man was caught up into paradise—whether in the body or out of the body I do not know, God knows—and he heard things that cannot be told.** (vv. 1–4a)

Paul heard things so awesome that we don't even know what he heard. He was like, *I can't even tell you! It would make your head explode. Okay? It was so* awesome *what I was told. I can't even tell you because I can't be responsible for your head!* Look at verse 5.

> **On behalf of this man I will boast, but on my own behalf I will not boast, except of my weaknesses. Though if I should wish to boast, I would not be a fool, for I would be speaking the truth. But I refrain from it, so that no one may think more of me than he sees in me or hears from me. So to keep me from becoming conceited because of the surpassing greatness of the revelations, a thorn was given me in the flesh, a messenger of Satan to harass me, to keep me from being conceited.** (vv. 5–7)

"Lest I should be exalted above measure" is the NKJV translation of Paul's explanation of why God allowed the thorn.

You're probably asking the question, *But was this really necessary? Doesn't it seem excessive?* And of course that's the question that Paul wanted to have answered.

Paul Pleads in Prayer.

"Three times I pleaded with the Lord about this, that it should leave me" (v. 8). If you know anything about prayer, this wasn't like he prayed at breakfast, lunch, and before lights out. He was referring to three extended seasons of prayer. The apostle is telling us, "I prayed and asked God to take it away and He didn't. So I went along for as far as I could and then I prayed again in another season and said, 'God, I can't take this anymore! I'm losing it over here! And You've got to take this away from me.' But God didn't.

"So I went on for another season, enduring and persevering. But then I couldn't take it anymore so I came back a third time! I cried, 'God! You have got to take this out of my life! It's too much for me!'"

And finally—not the first time, not the second time, but the third time—he got an answer.

Jesus Asks . . . and Submits.

Does that remind you of Jesus in the garden? He asked His Father, **"If it be possible, let this cup pass from Me. . . . If this cannot pass unless I drink it, your will be done. . . . He went away and prayed for the third time, saying the same words again"** (Matthew 26:39, 42, 44). I love that model of submission. Now Jesus got it done in three hours but nobody else is going to fast-track that process.

Do you remember what happened in the garden when the torches got lit and soldiers were coming to arrest Jesus? What did Peter do? He pulled out his sword and fought back. He was bad at fishing *and* at warring because I'm sure he wasn't going for the unfortunate soldier's ear (John 18:10).

But what's awesome is that after Jesus healed the soldier's ear, He turned to Peter and said, **"Shall I not drink the cup that the Father has given me?"** (John 18:11). Jesus was asking, "What else am I going to do? When it comes right down to it, everything I say I believe is on the line right now. There is no other choice. I'm going to keep going."

THE GRACE OF OUR LORD JESUS

Notice the answer that Paul gets and the answer that follows for us. **"But He said to me"** (v. 9). This is the only time in all of Paul's writings that he quotes Jesus. Acts 9:5 quotes Jesus speaking to Paul, but Paul himself never quotes Jesus speaking, except here, and about his thorn.

GOD'S GRACE IS

"But He said to me." That's in the perfect tense. It means that He said it and that settled it. Paul must have been hanging on to these words. *I have this. Jesus said it. It's done.*

THE PACKAGE

THAT ALL BLESSING

COMES IN.

"But He said to me, **'My grace is sufficient.'**" If you're going to get through with your thorn, you've got to have the grace. Your thorn will *crush* you without God's grace. Without grace, you will become bitter in a flash.

Let's just review a little bit about what God's Word says about this grace. God's grace is the package that all blessing comes in.

Romans 16:20 calls it the **"grace of our Lord Jesus Christ."** It's the best thing you can wish for someone else. Scripture repeats this blessing in 1 Thessalonians 5:28. Elsewhere the apostle Paul wishes his reader that **"the grace of our Lord Jesus Christ be with your spirit"** (Galatians 6:18; Philippians 4:23; Philemon 25) and **"the grace of our Lord Jesus Christ be with you all"** (2 Thessalonians 3:18).

"The grace of our Lord Jesus Christ be with you" because, without it, you are up a creek. You've got to get the grace. That grace we experience in salvation. In Acts 20:24 it's called **"the gospel of the grace of God."** Ephesians 2:8 says, **"For by grace you have been saved."**

But not just grace in salvation; grace in sanctification. Acts 13:43 tells how. "Paul and Barnabas, as they spoke with believers in Antioch, **"urged them to continue in the grace of God."** Paul wrote of that sanctifying grace to the Colossians, **"As you received Christ Jesus the Lord, so walk in him"** (Colossians 2:6). You can't walk unaided with the Lord anymore than you could save yourself in your own strength. "As you received the Lord"—helpless and broken—so walk in the Lord every day, taking that step of total dependence upon Him! The thorn, of course, promotes a deeper understanding of the extent of the grace of Jesus:

Grace in salvation.

Grace in sanctification.

Grace to serve. **"Having gifts that differ according to the grace given to us, let us use them"** (Romans 12:6). All that God provides you by His grace is ultimately the resources you have to serve Him.

And then, grace to be strong. 2 Timothy 2:1 says, **"Be strong in the grace"** (NKJV).

The familiar definition for grace is "unmerited favor," but it's so much more than that. Unmerited favor describes the source of grace but it doesn't really define it. What's grace for? What does it do?

Grace is the capacity to do anything spiritually profitable. You can't pray without grace. You can't understand the Bible without grace. You can't choose right over wrong without grace. You can't get through this thorn without grace. And that's why Jesus said to Paul, **"My grace is sufficient for you."** Those same words are meant for us. Stick with the grace of Jesus Christ all the way to eternity.

THE GRACE OF JESUS IS NOT FULLY SEEN UNTIL WEAKNESS IS FULLY EXPERIENCED.

Paul expressed astonishment that some were **"deserting him [God] who called you in the grace of Christ"** (Galatians 1:6). Exactly what I need to do is exactly what God wills for me to do—that's the grace. It's wisdom. It's strength. It's perseverance. It's discernment. It's faith. It's courage. It's confidence. It's comfort. It's conviction. Good things always comes as grace from God.

And notice *sufficient* in 2 Corinthians 12:9. The Greek word order here is fantastic. In the original language, the words are in this order: "Sufficient for you is the grace of Me." Jesus said, I am the grace.

Do you understand that God does not dispense strength and encouragement like a druggist fills a prescription? Do you get that? He's not like, "Here. Take two of these and call Me in the morning." He *is* the grace. He is the strength. It's intimacy with Him! His presence is power! No matter what we need, Jesus is the answer. "Sufficient for you is the grace of Me." *I am the grace!* He doesn't give it and then go on somewhere else like Santa dropping off presents. He comes to stay. **"I am with you always"** (Matthew 28:20).

Then notice, **"But he said to me, 'My grace is sufficient for you, for my power is made perfect in weakness'"** (v. 9). "Perfect" means fulfilled; accomplished; completed; finished. It's the same term Jesus spoke as His final word on the cross: *Tetelestai. It is finished.*

Notice also that God's grace is completed in our weakness. You never really get the grace unless you see the need for it. And even *that realization is* a grace. The grace of Jesus is not fully seen until weakness is fully experienced.

NO TIME TO QUIT

I told you that I originally developed and taught this content while Kathy and I were in California getting my cancer treatments. Looking back, I remember how difficult it was to keep at it when the season itself was so difficult. Talking about trials during the worst trials of our life—tough. Teaching on trials while I'm in the boat in the storm. I remember delivering the content of this chapter on a day when the pressure of everything that was happening to me, to us, and in our family was excruciating. The last place in the world I wanted to be was on the platform in front of people. But I wrote in my journal that day: "Tough time is not quitting time."

The time that we need most to recommit ourselves to the things God has called us to is exactly when the times are toughest. Satan desires to have us so that he might sift us like wheat. Yet the Lord has promised that He will be with us in the hour of the trial.

So the trial continues—with no end in sight. But there's hope of it coming to an end. Thorns are not forever. I don't know where Paul's life ended up. After he wrote Second Corinthians, he wrote two more letters to Corinthian believers that we don't have. Maybe in a Fourth Corinthians he wrote something like, "This awesome thing happened. My thorn—it's gone!" But if God wanted us to know that, we'd know it. I hate the idea that thorns are forever. They may *seem* to go on forever but they won't.

LIVING WITH YOUR THORN

So how do I live with my thorn? Paul did two things that we can do, too.

1. Boast in Your Thorn to Experience Christ's Power.

You can boast in your thorn. *What?* Yeah. It means to brag about it; to glory in it. *James, my marriage is crumbling. My illness is chronic. My grief is crushing me. My thorn is sharp and, man, it's deep! And you want me to* brag *about it?* What does God want you to do? Do what God's Word says and what Paul does in exemplary fashion:

"Therefore I will boast all the more gladly of my weaknesses, so that the power of Christ may rest upon me" (v. 9). Now I really wrestled with this word *gladly*. I studied this for a long time. And the best illustration I can give you of what he means is what happened Saturday night to us Mac-Donald kids. My brothers and I would play hard all day until we were so filthy dirty that my mom would stop us one by one on the front porch when we came home. She'd make us take everything off—three boys in our whitey-tighties and walk straight to the bathtub! All day Saturday you could get as dirty as you wanted but by Saturday night, you had to be sparkling clean, ready to wear your best clothes on Sunday.

I dreaded that Saturday night bath. But as much as I hated it, a strange thing would happen. After mom would get me in the tub, she'd go do whatever she had to do and I'd forget about how much I was supposed to hate it. All of a sudden, I got the rubber ducky in the water and the little boats going and there'd be bubbles everywhere! And I'd put some more water in the tub when that got cold. I stayed in so long that my hands got wrinkly and an hour had gone by. Then Mom would come back and make me get out and I'd start to cry . . . which I'm sure just made her smile and shake her head.

When we embrace our hardship we will find ourselves rejoicing in the parts that are good.

You will recall from the introduction to this book that beyond the health concerns of these last three years, we've also had some other trials that have been such a valley for us. About two months ago we were seeing some relief in this area. God had really answered so much prayer.

I remember standing in a worship service, reflecting back on the depth that God had brought to my prayer life and the depth that God had brought to my time in God's Word and the testimony that I had to share and how these trials have altered me. The thought crossed my mind, *I'm not glad that they happened.* But I also sensed a tangible gratitude for how God has been growing me.

> FIVE ACTIONS CAN HELP YOU TO ACCEPT YOUR WEAKNESSES—EVEN TO BOAST IN YOUR PERSONAL TRIALS.

Then I remember a little quiver of anxiety. *I don't want to be that person anymore. I don't ever want to go back to the person I was before I went through this crucible.* That gave me a little bit of insight into what it means here.

Look at the text again: "Therefore I will boast all the more gladly of my weaknesses, so that the power of Christ may rest upon me." There's a power that comes through boasting in weakness. *Here are five actions that can help* you to accept your weaknesses—even to boast in your personal trials.

First, count your blessings. Counting your blessings is boasting in your thorn. The deeper the thorn and harder the trial, the sweeter will be the blessing. Recounting your blessings will necessitate sharing the hard circumstances in which God has shown Himself faithful again. You are boasting when you say, "God allowed this hard thing in my life . . . but look at all the good that has come from it!"

Second, elevate your prayer life. Let your thorn drive you to communicate with focus, with fervency, and with frequency in God's presence. There was a time in my life, I am ashamed to say, that I had been a pastor for more than a decade and I didn't know what it was to get on my face before God. I had never spilt any tears on the carpet. I can't say that anymore. I don't want to go back there—yes, it was easier; but it was emptier! I don't want to be that person anymore. I'm thankful at least for what God's done in me.

Third, lengthen and deepen your time in God's Word. No more little quiet times. No more, like, *Oh where's that little book I keep on the back of the commode? Where's* The Daily Crouton? *I like to read that little story and get a little snippet of something that I can think about for the next three minutes.* No more of that. Deepen your time in God's Word.

I can tell you what the book of Isaiah has meant to me recently. Chapter after chapter, poring over the pages. Writing in the margin, "Yes, Lord," and "Thank You, Lord," "Forgive me, Lord. And, "For Your glory, Lord." Find a passage of Scripture and go deeply into it and let it become your treasure. **"Oh how I love your law! It is my meditation all the day"** (Psalm 119:97).

Fourth, tell your story to people. That's how you can boast in your weakness; tell people what God's doing. There's a subtle but important difference between boasting and bragging in the sense that Paul was using. He was echoing the words of Jeremiah 9:23–24, "Thus says the Lord, 'Let not the wise man boast in his wisdom, let not the mighty man boast in his might, let not the rich man boast in his riches, but let him who boasts boast in this, that he understands and knows me, that I am the Lord who practices steadfast love, justice, and righteousness in the earth. For in these things I delight,' declares the Lord."

Telling your story isn't about you being the hero but you gladly being a weak person through whom God works. God doesn't have to add His power to our power—we have none! God displays His power through our weakness, and the people in our lives will be drawn to Him when we let them know that we realize what He is accomplishing in and through us in spite of our weaknesses. So tell people what God is doing in your life!

Fifth, focus on the prize. Keep reminding yourself where this is all going and where we're all going to be in about ten more minutes. Eternity is racing upon us this moment! We are locked in time. From our perspective, God's plan seems to be working itself out so slowly, but forever is *rocketing* toward us.

So **"set your minds on things that are above, not on things that are on earth. For you have died, and your life is hidden with Christ in God"** (Colossians 3:2–3). Your thorn will not go with you when you cross the finish line!

Paul was always about the Day. **"I know whom I have believed, and I am convinced that He is able to guard until that Day what has been entrusted to me"** (2 Timothy 1:12). **"Henceforth there is laid up for me the crown of righteousness which the Lord, the righteous judge, will award to me on that Day"** (2 Timothy 4:8). Paul couldn't wait for it. Focus on the prize.

So boast in your thorn to experience Christ's power.

2. Be Content in Your Thorn to Experience Christ's Purpose.

"For the sake of Christ, then, I am content" (v. 10). Now, that does not mean that I like the thorn; that I want it; or that I enjoy it. Don't accept that kind of pressure from people who twist platitudes from Scripture. But I accept it. I submit to it. And I embrace it. By God's grace, I rest in it. I'm not putting my life on hold. I'm not counting the seconds until the thorn is removed. I'm not getting by and refusing to enjoy anything else. God help me. I'm living my life with the thorn. The choice may not be easy, but the alternatives are all much harder in the long run!

"For the sake of Christ, then, I am content with weaknesses" (v. 10). The NKJV translates weaknesses as "infirmities," meaning, I am content with thorns that are physical trials. But Paul went beyond, as if knowing how much help we would need, and listed off various kinds of thorns for which he was willing to be content.

I am content with thorns that are **"insults"** (v. 10) or **"reproaches"** (NKJV). Those are relational thorns, the intentional and unintentional barbs that others inflict on us.

I am content with thorns that are **"hardships"** (v. 10). These are lasting trials dealing with financial and material matters. The NKJV uses the term *necessities* for these material thorns—bankruptcy, foreclosure, even poverty.

I am content with thorns that are **"persecutions"** (v. 10). I am content with personal attacks. These are spiritual thorns—suffering for the name of Christ.

I am content with thorns that are **"calamities"** (v. 10). That means literally distresses. Emotional thorns—fear, anxiety, and personal disasters.

How Paul? How are you content with these things? How could he speak that way of insults, hardships, persecutions, and calamities?

His answer is right at the beginning of verse 10: "For the sake of Christ."

Why can we be content during hardships and calamities? Because we love Christ so much. Because we know He is the purpose of our existence, the reason we are here. It's His glory and His fame that we're living for.

He's in control of the details. And if He has *allowed* this thorn to come into our lives and He says to you and to me as He said to the apostle Paul, "My grace is sufficient for you, for my power [my presence] is made perfect in weakness" (v. 9).

So let's boast in the thorn to experience Christ's power. Let's be content with the thorn to experience Christ's purpose.

CHANGED BY THE THORN

Does anybody remember their childhood sweetheart? My wife is so amazing. Apart from salvation, she's God's greatest gift to me. But I have to tell the truth. Kathy was not my first love . . .

I was in first grade and her name was Wendy. She went to our church. She had two brothers and every week we used to carpool together to Boys Brigade Club. And every week I hoped Wendy would be in the car.

I would follow her around at Sunday School and peek behind the curtains that portioned off all of the classrooms to catch a look at her. I don't ever remember talking to her, I just remember thinking she was *so* cute.

I also remember that she got very sick with cancer. I was in first grade and didn't really understand all that was happening. Eventually she was in the car every time we'd be going back-and-forth to Brigade. I'm sure her mother needed the relief, so she would ride with her father. I remember when she lost her hair. I had never told anyone about my crush, but I would sit in the backseat and I would see her and think about her. I was puzzled by all of it.

She got sicker and sicker and then sadly, Wendy died. I remember her funeral. I remember not getting it at all and being afraid to be around people who were experiencing such grief and not having any idea what it was all about.

Wendy's mother's name was Bernice. She used to sing in a trio at our church. I can remember that after a few months, she began singing again. For years after, whenever I saw her mother sing, I would always think of Wendy.

Bernice was changed by this thorn. Before Wendy's sickness and death, Bernice had become estranged from her nonbelieving family. For years, she hadn't even talked to them. But I'm sure it was her grief over losing Wendy that changed all of that. That loss was her thorn. She began to reach out to her parents and to her brothers.

She reached out to one brother specifically. She invited him to come to church on a Sunday night and hear her sing. She would have never done that before her thorn—never! But she did it now. And he came. And he brought his teenage daughter with him and she started to attend our youth group on a regular basis. Eventually that niece gave her life to Christ.

I know that whole story, of course, because Bernice's niece—the daughter who came and got saved—is my wife, Kathy.

Now I'm not saying for a moment that God gave Wendy cancer, and least of all, so Kathy could get saved. I don't understand it all. I just know that God promises that **"all things work together for good to those who love God** (Romans 8:28 NKJV). And that His grace is sufficient for you and me and His strength is made perfect in weakness.

Prayer of Commitment

Father, I realize now that just because I know that thorns last and that You want to bring great good out of my thorn doesn't mean that my thorn will now be removed. I want to accept the fact that this may be the first in many lessons You want me to "get" from this thorn. But for now, I need Your grace desperately not to be a quitter. I need to remember that Your grace, not my strength will carry me through.

Father, You can receive glory by my crowns and also by my thorns. Either way, Lord, be glorified in my life. Let me count even the painful lessons as blessings from Your hands.

Lord, I realize that elevating my prayer life and deepening my time in Your Word are two sides of the same conversation. Help me hear You speak in such a way that I am drawn to You. I know You want Your Word to have that effect in my life.

And about that thorn, Lord. You allowed it for Your purposes and I long to see Your purposes fulfilled in my life. In Jesus' name, Who is my sufficient grace, Amen.

FROM GOD'S HEART TO MINE:

2 Corinthians 12:9–11

"My grace is sufficient for you, for my power is made perfect in weakness." Therefore I will boast all the more gladly of my weaknesses, so that the power of Christ may rest upon me. For the sake of Christ, then, I am content with weaknesses, insults, hardships, persecutions, and calamities. For when I am weak, then I am strong.

James 1:12

Blessed is the man who remains steadfast under trial, for when he has stood the test he will receive the crown of life.

MINING FOR GOLD

1. Pause and again use the prayer at the end of the chapter to slow down. Ask God to help you keep trusting Him even if your trial seems like a never-ending thorn right now.

2. What trials in your life do you think might turn out to be "thorns" as the apostle Paul defined them?

3. Until now, how have you been responding to them? As trials or thorns?

4. Using Paul as an example (2 Corinthians 12:7–11), what changes in your view and handling of the thorn(s) need to be made?

5. So far, what examples of good have you seen come from your thorns or the thorns of others?

6. In what ways and places are you able to "boast" about your thorns? When will you do that?

But he knows the way that I take;
when he has tried me, **I shall come out as gold.** Job 23:10

God Refines

This trial will draw sin out of my life.

Well, we've saved the best part for last: **"I shall come out as gold."** This picture of the completed refining process pulls the whole verse together. Allow me to give you a lesson in Gold 101.

When gold is being refined, it first must be melted. Gold ore is mixed with other metals and impurities when it comes out of the ground. So they crank up the furnaces to 1010 degrees Celsius, the temperature at which gold melts.

The second process is binding. Once the gold is molten, they mix in a special flux to make it more fluid and to bind the impurities together. Then, when they pour the gold into a mold, the impurities, called slag, rise to the top.

Lastly, they separate it. After the gold has cooled, the slag is broken off and the steps are repeated—sometimes multiple times for greater purity. This process hasn't changed in thousands of years. Technology hasn't improved it. God has given us a lasting illustration of His methods with us.

That's what's in Job's mind as he wrote, **"And when He has tried me, I shall come out as gold."** This trial is refining you. Do you feel the heat? Do you feel the slag rising to the top? The biblical word for slag is *sin* and it's what makes you restless and miserable and fearful and selfish. Is God drawing the impurities in your life to the surface?

Some people go into the furnace of affliction and it burns them; others go in, and the experience purifies them. If you submit to the Lord, as painful as the crisis may be, it will refine you and make you better. If you resist what God is doing, the furnace will only scorch you.

If the trial is making your faith purer and stronger and you're not bitter toward the Lord but are loving Him more, then, no doubt about it, you are coming out as gold.

Some people go into the furnace of affliction and it burns them;
others go in, and the experience purifies them.
What's the difference?

CHAPTER 6

COME FORTH AS
GOLD

M y mother has always displayed an amazing sense of humor, just one of many outstanding characteristics that make me intensely proud as her son. For years, my mother had as many as a hundred elementary school children packed into her basement on Tuesday afternoons to teach them Bible stories. She ran an after-school program in our school district that gave kids a dynamic first exposure to God's Word.

I can remember as a student at that same elementary school seeing my mother passing out flyers to students inviting them over at the end of the day. I confess that at the time I was a little embarrassed, but now I see what an example she was to me. I am proud to be her son. Over the years, she led to Christ many of the women in the neighboring homes. She had them over for coffee, befriended them, and then introduced them to her best friend, Jesus. She was doing friendship evangelism when Joe Aldrich, author of *Lifestyle Evangelism*, was in diapers!

Part of her winsomeness was always her sense of humor. But in 2008 I noticed that she didn't seem to be able to control her laughter. She would keep going when everyone else stopped. She'd laugh over jokes at odd times and in odd ways. I sensed things weren't quite right. By the time we were leaving to California for my cancer treatments, Mom's speech was beginning to be affected. She complained regularly of a sore throat. Then her words became hard to understand. I found myself thinking *What?* when she spoke, and often I asked her to repeat what she had said.

My dad arranged for her to see a doctor and get some tests. We guessed she might have strained the nerves in her neck. At first the doctors were baffled. There was obviously a problem, but they couldn't figure out what it was. After several terrifying guesses, like ALS, a diagnosis was confirmed that she has a condition called bulbar palsy. Unlike ALS, a motor neuron disease with symptoms that start in the extremities and work toward the core, these symptoms appear in the central region from the bottom of your nose to the chest area.

Mom's condition worsened. Her garbled speech increased to the point of being completely unintelligible. Her mind was fully functioning, but we couldn't make sense of what she was trying to say. She was now also choking on food and had great difficulty in swallowing. She lost control of expressions like laughing and crying, so that she would sometimes laugh a brief time, followed by a sudden switch to crying. These motor-neuron issues were difficult to observe and even harder on her—someone who had always been so dynamic, full of life and good humor.

Much of Mom's role throughout her adult years has involved talking. She has participated in marriage seminars and taught children. Her voice had quality to it. Not long ago, she played for us a DVD that she recorded awhile back for the eightieth anniversary of our church growing up. She hadn't been a member for years, but those organizing the celebration wanted to record her testimony because they knew the impact she would make. Her voice had been such a familiar sound in all parts of that congregation. She had come to Christ and grown there and served there for several decades. Listening to her voice brought back so many great memories.

I'm writing this half a year later, and her condition has gradually deteriorated. She now has a surgically implanted feeding tube to avoid aspirating her food. Though the prognosis is clear, my mother will not give way without a fight. I have never seen Mom more joyful than in our recent visits. She smiles happily and doesn't let her limitations bother her. She gleefully wields her pad of paper and writes down things she wants others to "hear" from her. She continues to teach and express her perspective, engaging people around her. We recently had a family reunion and Mom managed to be the center of it all, a godly woman in her prime, enjoying the company of the generations to which she is leaving a great heritage.

You may have noticed that I dedicated this book to my mother. It is my prayer that she will live to see these chapters in print. She is a vibrant example of what it means to count it all joy. Her trying time is certainly not over, but I can see the gold in her that God has patiently refined.

WHEN *YOUR* LIFE IS HARD

Counting our trials as joy is only one of the many truths we've learned in our study of trials. It's hard to absorb them all in one brushstroke. Depending on where you are in your walk with Christ and specifically where you are in your season of difficulty, these truths have hit you in different ways. And if you would read all this again next month, you would probably find yourself in yet another place. Praise God that our feet are not stuck in mud but running hard after God and all that He has for us.

So, before we close up this book, I want to make sure that you have these lessons for yourself. We need to place these truths into our hearts and into our heads to remind ourselves what to think and believe as we walk through the times when life is hard.

Let these truths nourish your soul. You just flat out need to have them . . .

• when crazy thoughts steal your sleep in the middle of the night.

• when an unexpected storm threatens your home or your future or your loved ones.

• when what you thought was safe is hijacked by someone else's sin.

• when God enrolls you in some graduate-level course in character development.

In these times and countless more, these principles can't be far from your mind.

As a matter of review, these are the Scriptures that we have repeatedly turned to in our study:

1 Peter 4   James 1   Hebrews 12   2 Corinthians 12

Essentially, these four passages repeat four main truths about how to turn your trials to gold. In this chapter, we'll focus on each of these four principles as they occur in each of these four passages.

That's 4 principles x 4 passages = 16 lessons

Got it? I pray this creative review will help you better absorb these powerful truths as I prayerfully put them before you. Take your time reviewing each one. Review them for your own personal reality, not just for head knowledge. Ask the Lord to help you to plant them in your life—vibrant, alive, real truth beating in your heart and walking with you each day. Return to them often when you find yourself wanting hard to escape the place where God has positioned you for this season.

The first of the four principles appears on the next page.

PRINCIPLE 1

Every trial I face is allowed by God
for my ultimate good.

Every trial I face is allowed by God for my ultimate good. For my *good.*
Say it out loud: "For *my good."*

This truth is the rock our feet need to be on when the waves of satanic lies attempt to sweep us under. Say it again: "This trial that I'm going through . . . is *for my ultimate good."*

This truth is the anchor that I can hold on to in the storm.

This truth is the wind that fills my sails of hope.

This truth is the light that guides my ship of faith safely into the harbor.

Every trial I face is allowed by God for my ultimate good.

Now let's qualify that principle a bit more with four key lessons.

LESSON 1

Every *trial* I face is allowed by God for my ultimate good:
Trials, not consequences.

| 1 Peter 4 | James 1 |
| Hebrews 12 | 2 Corinthians 12 |

WHERE DID THIS PAIN COME FROM?

"Am I suffering in a trial, or is my pain a consequence of something I've done?" You need to identify the source of that hard thing in your life because your responsibility in the matter depends on the source of your hardship. First Peter 4:14 says, **"If you are insulted for the name of Christ, you are blessed, because the Spirit of glory and of God rests upon you."**

What brought on this hardship? Is the difficulty you're enduring a wake-up call to the reality of your bad choices, or has it been allowed by God to train your character?

A painful consequence is something you reap when you plant a seed full of sin—something harmful you've done, harsh words you've spoken, places you've gone, wrong priorities you've pursued, commitments you've neglected, or selfish choices you've made. If you are today harvesting heartache from a sin you've previously planted, then humbly repent of your actions right now.

Many believers are experiencing very painful consequences to sin in their lives. They may call those consequences trials, but **"do not be deceived,"** Galatians 6:7 says. **"God is not mocked, for whatever one sows, that will he also reap."**

Look at the following four situations. Which is a trial? Which is a consequence?

"My marriage is in trouble after many years of neglect."

"My husband lost his job because the automobile industry is suffering."

"My husband lost his job because he stole a bunch of stuff from work."

"My son has a serious illness and is in the hospital."

The answers: (1) consequence; (2) trial; (3) consequence; (4) trial for you, possible consequence for him.

Continuing in 1 Peter 4 is this warning of consequence: **"But let none of you suffer as a murderer or a thief or an evildoer or as a meddler"** (v. 15). And then Peter defines trial: **"Yet if anyone suffers as a Christian, let him not be ashamed, but let him glorify God in that name"** (v. 16).

"Murderer" describes anyone with a hateful action or thought—who disrespects life.

"Thief" describes anyone who loses his or her job for stealing time; anyone who loses his or her marriage for stealing selfish interests; anyone who loses his or her friend by stealing too much attention. All of these actions involve taking what belongs to someone else.

"Evildoer" is a general term for describing anyone who participates in sinful activity.

"Meddler" describes anyone who, as one translation puts it, is "prying into other people's affairs" (NLT). If any of these descriptions is what's causing your hardship, you're suffering a consequence, not a trial. In His kindness, God promises that trials will come. It's true that we are forgiven the penalty of sin, but we still must suffer the harvest of consequences. Wrong actions have wrong consequences, even for Christians. God will make sure of it.

I'll say it again, if you're suffering consequences, repent right now. Turn around and—don't walk—*run* back to God.

_____

_____

_____

_____

_____

_____

LESSON 2

Every trial I face is allowed by God for my ultimate *good:*
Good = all I need is not all I want.

1 Peter 4   James 1

Hebrews 12   2 Corinthians 12

NEEDS VERSUS WANTS

It's highly doubtful that the Rolling Stones ever intended to teach a biblical principle in their song lyrics to "You Can't Always Get What You Want." But they're right: You don't get what you want, "but . . . you get what you need." That's what James 1:2–4 tells us that God gives us in our trials. He gives us what we need.

That's why James writes, **"Count it all joy . . . when you fall into various trials . . . And let steadfastness have its full effect,** *that you may be perfect and complete, lacking in nothing"* (italics added).

One of the great pains of life is that things are not always the way we want them to be. But get this, God makes sure that everything we need, we have. Everything we want, we do not have. When the Scripture says that God is working everything out for our ultimate good (Romans 8:28), that doesn't mean that we're going to have everything we want. As James 1:4 says, our steadfastness (our endurance) leads to us being "perfect," "complete," and "lacking in nothing." What great terms!

Perfect—we will have all the character we need to honor God.

Complete—we will have all the relationships we need to nourish and sustain us.

Lacking in nothing—we will miss out on nothing that would give us 100 percent satisfaction in God.

If I am perfect and complete, lacking in nothing—then I have everything I need to do everything God wants me to do. I can show the world the superiority of the life lived in God.

Every trial I face is allowed by God for my ultimate good. In part, that good includes my ability to discern the difference between needs and wants. Today if I endure, God promises to give me what I need. Tomorrow, in heaven, He promises to give me everything I could ever want and more.

For now, let's be thankful and content. You and I have everything we need to do everything that God wants us to do.

LESSON 3

Every trial I face is allowed by God for my *ultimate* good:
Ultimate, not immediate.

1 Peter 4   James 1

 Hebrews 12   2 Corinthians 12

IT TAKES TIME

Might I remind us all that we are not the first Christians who have ever lived. The whole "walk by faith, not by sight" adventure has been going on for dozens and dozens of generations. Five hundred years ago there were people who thought they were the first to face trials like we do today. They thought their experiences were new just like we think ours are new—even as the mothballs are gathering around our feet. The pages of church history are filled with people who have drawn down on the truths that we're talking about right now and proven God faithful in their generation. You're going to do the same.

These, our faithful predecessors of faith, would tell you if they could that the trial that you face today will turn out to be for your ultimate good. It may not seem so today but, really, it will.

I love the honesty of Hebrews 12:11: "For the moment all discipline seems painful rather than pleasant." Discipline seems painful because it is, but **"later it yields the peaceful fruit of righteousness."** If you're patient, there's fruit coming, like a farmer in a field harvesting a crop long after he planted the seed.

Do you already see the peaceable fruit of righteousness growing in your life? Do you see yourself changed by God's training? Of course that growth is conditional to you cooperating with what God is doing. The good that God is bringing to your life can be seen only through the perspective of time.

This trial is for your transformation, so that you might stand in that long line of generations of Christians—"so great a cloud of witnesses," says Hebrews 12:1—who would shout out to you today, "Keep going. Good is coming. It'll all be worth it. Don't give up! Look to Jesus."

LESSON 4

Every trial I face is *allowed* by God for my ultimate good:
Allowed, not caused.

1 Peter 4	James 1
Hebrews 12	2 Corinthians 12

TURNING IT AROUND FOR GOOD

With all due respect to Rabbi Kushner, God does allow bad things to happen to good people. He doesn't *cause* them, but He doesn't prevent them either. The world is free and God doesn't very often step in and alter the fact that the effects of sin are visiting themselves randomly upon the creation. So God lets trials happen to Christians just like He lets them happen to the pagans so that the superiority of the life lived in God can be demonstrated. The majority of the world is choosing not to worship God, but a few of us, by God's grace, can draw down upon God's promised resources to get us through.

God did not cause the horrible events in your life, but you need to embrace the fact that He allowed them. God could not make a world in which we are free and at the same time guarantee that everyone would choose Him. So the world is broken and bad things happen. But God promises that He will be with those who love Him. He will bring us through the fire, and we will come forth as gold.

God allowed Paul to suffer a "thorn . . . in the flesh." Paul said that God allowed **"a messenger of Satan to harass me, to keep me from becoming conceited"** (2 Corinthians 12:7). Paul understood that God allowed this pain in his life for a reason. God allowed a demon "to harass," or "buffet" (NKJV) Paul. The word *buffet* means *to strike with a fist or beat.* But God permitted it with a purpose: to keep the apostle from being conceited.

God is always sovereign. He is so much in control that even when Satan tries to ruin our lives, God takes the weapon that Satan wants to use to destroy us and turns it into a good thing. God says, "If you will lean hard on Me in the midst of this difficult time, I'll take that thorn and make it for your good."

We all have a thorn. We all have something that God has allowed into our lives that Satan meant for our destruction but that God has turned around to help us grow and change. God, help us again today to choose to trust You with it.

PRINCIPLE 2:
Trials need not steal my joy.

I was not a great youth pastor. One of the reasons why I was so lame was because I hate theme parks. Even more than theme parks, I hate roller coasters.

I could take you to places all around North America where kids talked me into riding on crazy, convoluted, death-defying, twisting roller coasters. I've left more vomit on more rides and riders than I can count. Just how ashamed do you think I felt looking at those kids' faces? I could tell you a lot of stories. Needless to say, I'll never ride a roller coaster *ever* again!

But I have a confession to make: Even though I don't ride roller coasters anymore, sometimes I make the foolish choice to get on an emotional roller coaster. It used to be that on any given day I was doing good and then something bad happened and I went into the tank. Then there was good news—but wait; then there was bad news—no wait, we're okay again. I rode emotional highs, lows, and corkscrews. That's an awful way to live. I've come to the place now where I acknowledge that trials need not steal my joy.

I'm not trying to hammer someone who has lost their joy today. But I'm telling you, it doesn't have to be that way and I want to show you why. You can get off the roller coaster. I can, too. We can focus on the presence and power of God in any circumstance.

This trial need not steal my joy.

LESSON 5

Trials need not steal my joy . . .
because they bring me to the power of God.

1 Peter 4	James 1
Hebrews 12	2 Corinthians 12

STRENGTH IN WEAKNESS

How do people do it? How do they withstand the Katrina-like blows that pummel their lives? The wind, the waves, the surges of heartbreak, one after another. How do they survive . . . and still lift their faces to the Lord? How can they be so strong at their extreme weakest?

I know the answer. I know it well because I'm personally living it. Working through the truths of God's Word as it relates to trials, I feel like I'm the farmer in the field harvesting the crops in the afternoon and putting them on the table for supper that night. All that I am sharing with you is fresh from the field. I'm in it. I'm living it.

I'm writing this on an awful day. Some very heavy things have hit Kathy and me off balance. But somewhere in the middle of that storm, God's voice is telling me that He provides sufficient grace for this trial, and when I am weak, He is always very strong. So I want to say to the glory of God that if there is anything in this book that is powerful, it is from weakness. **"Therefore I will boast all the more gladly of my weaknesses, so that the power of Christ may rest upon me. . . . For when I am weak, then I am strong"** (2 Corinthians 12:9–10). It's the hard times and the unhealthy times and the hurting times that reveal my weaknesses. And it's also during those times that God shows up strong.

We often treat suffering like a dodgeball game. Anytime anything hard comes at us, we jump out of the way. We spend our whole lives trying to avoid anything that will hurt or be hard. But there's a better kind of life— a deeper, more fulfilling kind of life—that isn't about avoiding every pain.

It's about finding God faithful and powerful in the midst of whatever trials or thorns He allows.

There's something about our weakness that opens the flow of God's strength. In the midst of a trial, there's a power coming into your life that you've never experienced before.

When you see a hard thing coming, try saying, *I may not want this, but I know I'm going to see Christ working in my life in an incredible way.*

God never allows a thorn without providing sufficient grace and strength in our weaknesses. Sufficient grace is not just enough to survive, but enough to have supernatural joy in the midst of anything He allows us to go through.

LESSON 6

Trials need not steal my joy . . .
because they prove I am God's child.

| 1 Peter 4 | James 1 |
| | 2 Corinthians 12 |

ALL GOD'S KIDS ARE GETTING IT

The road you walk today through your trial is different than the dark road your non-Christian neighbors travel. They have no concept of what's going on in their lives, what it means, or where it's going. The fact that you're going through difficult days and you're not bitter but you're better and you love the Lord more—all of that is proof positive that you're a card-carrying member of the family of God.

How much good news is that?! You're part of God's family. You're one of his daughters; I'm one of His sons. We're His children.

Maybe you're reading all this about trials but thinking, *I don't know what you're talking about. Everything is humming along in my life and it has been that way for a decade now. No problems of any kind: money in the bank; no health crisis; kids are perfect; marriage is rocking!* Well, that's not good news, because Hebrews 12:5–7 says that all God's kids are getting it! So if you're not going through any trials, you better return to "Go" and find out if you're really in the family.

But if you are in the family, you're getting a lot of amazing things coming your way. First John 3:1 says, **"See what kind of love the Father has given to us, that we should be called children of God."**

As a child of God:

• You get hell canceled. (That would be amazing even if that was it!)

• You get heaven guaranteed.

• You get the Spirit of God as the deposit that the rest of God's blessing is coming.

• You get the assurance of the forgiveness of sin.

• You get the glory of Christian fellowship.

(Hebrews 12:6). If you're in a trial, see it as proof of God's love for you. **"For the Lord disciplines the one he loves, and chastises every son whom he receives."**

Let me be loud and clear and speak that truth into your heart: God loves you.

His eyes are upon you every moment. You are never out of His thoughts. The Lord tells His people, **"I have loved you with an everlasting love"** (Jeremiah 31:3). Paul reminds us that nothing **"will be able to separate us from the love of God in Christ Jesus our Lord"** (Romans 8:39). You didn't do anything to deserve His love; you don't do anything to maintain it. God has chosen to set His love on you, not because of who you are but because of who He is. He is your Father and you are His child.

LESSON 7

Trials need not steal my joy . . .
because they increase my endurance

1 Peter 4	James 1
Hebrews 12	2 Corinthians 12

PROTECT YOUR JOY

This matter of endurance is critical to the Christian life. James 1 tells us that above all other human traits, endurance is the characteristic that God is trying to build into your life and mine. This is perseverance, steadfastness. We need to make and keep the commitments of life. No matter how hard it seems, don't quit. You will develop endurance only by enduring.

Endurance is the funnel through which all Christian virtue flows. If God can just get me to not be a quitter, He can get every other good thing into my life. If I won't quit my marriage and I won't quit my kids and I won't quit my job and I won't quit my church, God will accomplish great things.

Instead of thinking the grass is greener somewhere else, we must believe, *This is where God has me! This is where I'm going to put down roots and plant my life and make a difference;* if I'll stay right here under the pressure, it's unbelievable what God could do in my life. But we've got to be willing to commit for the long haul in order for God's trials to have their purpose in our lives.

James tells us, **"Blessed is the man who remains steadfast under trial, for when he has stood the test he will receive the crown of life"** (1:12). While I think there are literal crowns that we'll receive from the Lord, I'd like to suggest that the "crown of life" means the quality of life that God promises to those who love Him. If you endure, if you stand the test, there'll be a better life for you on the other side of this trial. Your best and most fruitful days are ahead. Your most God-glorifying days are ahead. God has a purpose in this trial, and if you hold up under it, you're going to receive the "crown of life." It's a quality of life that comes to those who successfully pass the test—those who love Him. For some people it will be in eternity, but for most people it'll be at some point later in this life.

Protect your joy—remain under the pressure and don't let this trial steal what's ahead.

_____

_____

_____

_____

_____

_____

_____

_____

_____

_____

_____

_____

_____

_____

_____

_____

_____

_____

_____

_____

_____

_____

LESSON 8

Trials need not steal my joy . . .
because they build my intimacy with Jesus.

1 Peter 4   James 1
Hebrews 12   2 Corinthians 12

A NEW CONNECTION WITH THE LORD

Recently I was reading through a stack of my old journals. In these note-books I've kept a chronicle of my own relationship with God and all the things that He's been teaching me over the years. When you go back and look at these records, you'd think that the sweetest times with the Lord would be the times of greatest victory. But that's not the case. The frequency of entries and the intimacy of fellowship are so much more apparent during times of hardship.

Why is that? Why is it that Christ seems so near during times of hardship?" It's **"the fellowship of His sufferings"** that Philippians 3:10 talks about. Does Jesus know about suffering? Yes, He does. So when we suffer, we feel an affinity with Him. Through hardship is a way that He draws near to us like in no other way; as Hebrews 4 says, **"He's touched with the feelings of our infirmities."**

First Peter 4:13 says, **"But rejoice insofar as you share Christ's sufferings, that you may also rejoice and be glad when his glory is revealed."** "Rejoice . . . rejoice." Twice in one verse, in the middle of a discussion on suffering, we're told to rejoice. But the second requires the first; if we *rejoice* in the sufferings we can expect to rejoice in the revelation of His glory!

Why would I rejoice in my suffering?

Here's why: You share in Christ's suffering. You have a new understanding and new connection with Jesus. Some people say this verse is talking about a future time when we'll be glad when His glory is revealed to the world. It could also mean that we'll be glad when His glory is revealed in us—that we'll rejoice when we look in the mirror and see a different person, because the glory of Christ will be more revealed through our lives. Both options are pretty cool, and we can hold out this truth either way: there's a closeness with the Lord that comes through trials that doesn't come any other way. Rejoice in this opportunity.

PRINCIPLE 3
God is never more present than when
His children are suffering.

Get your arms around this really important truth: God is never more present in your life than when you are suffering. The harder the trial, the closer He moves toward you. Are you feeling crushed today? He is rushing toward you to stand beside you and help you.

You're like, "That's not what I'm feeling right now. I'm right in the middle of something hard and it feels like God has left me."

Well, I guess it depends on what you think God's goals are.

If you believe that God exists to make you comfortable, then you will find Him very absent in your discomfort.

If you believe that God exists to make your life run smoothly, then you will find God very absent when your life hits a rocky patch.

If you believe that God exists to make you happy, then you will find God very absent when your heart is broken and your tears are flowing.

But—and I love this *but*—if you believe as the Scripture teaches that God's goal is to make you holy, then right where you are in the center of your hardship, you will feel His arms around you. Through every intense, heart-wrenching moment of this trial, God's presence has and will become increasingly real.

To have a right view of God, consider what He's doing in this trial. He's at work in your life even as a master craftsman works his art. You feel Him at work like a house feels a carpenter; like a sculpture feels the sculptor; like a painting feels the artist—hammered, chiseled, and brushed.

Receive the next four pictures of how God describes His nearness to you in this trial. We start again at the top of our list of four Scripture passages.

LESSON 9

God is never more present than when His children are suffering.
He is an experienced sufferer, fellowshiping with me.

1 Peter 4   James 1

Hebrews 12   2 Corinthians 12

JESUS STANDS FOR YOU

Jesus Christ is an experienced sufferer. Lest you hold in your mind a picture of an anemic, weak Jesus, replace it with this: Jesus has His PhD in suffering. He has suffered like no other for your sin and mine. Not only does He *identify* with your suffering, but He is *present* with you in your suffering. First Peter 4:14 says, **"If you are insulted for the name of Christ, you are blessed, because the Spirit of glory and of God rests upon you."**

There's a unique intimacy with Christ when you're suffering for Him. It's unlike anything else. Think of Stephen in Acts 7 when he was giving up his life for Christ. As the crowd began to stone him, Stephen **"gazed into heaven and saw the glory of God, and Jesus standing at the right hand of God"** (v. 55). If you're a careful Bible student, you'd question, *Why was Jesus standing? Hebrews makes such a big deal about how "he sat down at the right hand of the Majesty on high"* (1:3). Yet in this glimpse into glory, Stephen, at the moment of his greatest suffering, saw Jesus standing for him.

Jesus rose in honor, welcome, and identification with Stephen. As we've already seen, this new intimacy with Christ includes **"the fellowship of His sufferings"** (Philippians 3:10 NASB). Believe by faith that in the middle of your trials you are experiencing the fellowship of God's presence that gives you new courage to not give up. *I'm not going to lose my faith, God help me. I'm going to keep on. I'm going to serve Him until I get there.* In such moments of faith, there's a wave of grace that God rushes upon you.

How do you keep this wave in motion? Keep your communication open with the Lord. I'm not talking casual prayers over the shoulder. I mean on your face before God—a posture that we've had too little of in our lives. And in that place, the Lord will meet you. If you will humble yourself, the Lord will be present with you. He is an experienced sufferer, fellowshiping with you.

God is never more present than when His children are suffering. Draw near.

LESSON 10

God is never more present than when His children are suffering.
He is an attentive counselor, listening with me.

1 Peter 4   James 1

Hebrews 12   2 Corinthians 12

JESUS LISTENS

What do you think about prayer? Do you think that God really wants to talk to you? Do you think He really wants to hear what is on your heart?

The answer is, *Yes, He really does.* He is an attentive counselor who listens to you in your trials. You understand this picture if you know what it's like to sit and talk to someone who really knows how to listen. That guy heard you. That girl gets it. You can see in their eyes that they're tracking with you.

Psalm 116:1–2 says, **"I love the Lord, because He has heard my cries. Because He bends down and listens."** Picture your closest friend, turning his ear to you, and you cup your hand around your mouth and whisper your need. That's the picture.

God knows exactly what's going on in your life. He's aware of your needs and your heartaches and your worries about the future. *God totally gets it—* that one truth has inspired and comforted God's people through thousands of years of history.

Not only is God listening to your prayer, but He will also give you wisdom about your trial if you ask Him for it. James 1:5 tells us, **"If any of you lacks wisdom, let him ask God, who gives generously to all without reproach, and it will be given him."** That phrase "without reproach" means literally that God won't sink His teeth into you. God won't say, "What? What are you asking Me that for!?" He's not the impatient parent who doesn't have time for you or the irritable boss who snaps back. No, He's the attentive counselor, listening to you.

Take to heart the comfort of Psalm 62:8: **"Trust in him at all times, O people; pour out your heart before him; God is a refuge for us."**

_____

_____

_____

_____

_____

_____

_____

_____

_____

_____

_____

_____

_____

_____

_____

_____

_____

_____

_____

_____

_____

_____

_____

_____

_____

LESSON 11

God is never more present than when His children are suffering.
He is a loving Father, chastening me.

1 Peter 4	James 1
Hebrews 12	2 Corinthians 12

FOR MY GOOD

I would have been a better behaved kid if I could have been a parent first.

Kids just don't understand what parents try to do for them. If you're a parent, don't you wish that your kids could see that every action that you take toward them, even imperfectly, is out of love? But they don't always get that.

When I was an adolescent, I remember thinking my parents were so confused. Then I grew up and, as Mark Twain mused, I was amazed at how much they had learned.

I thought it was hard when I had to discipline my kids when they were young. Little kids are quite a handful. When your kids get older and you must let them experience the consequences of their choices, they become quite a "heartful." Especially when you can't step in and keep the pain from happening. You have to watch them suffer the cost of their decisions. For sure, heartful is harder than handful.

How is it with you today? Are you in a trial as a discipline from your loving Father? Do you feel His sadness that it had to come to this in order for you to learn? I don't want to get older and still be an adolescent Christian. I want to grow up in the Lord and trust my heavenly Father even when I don't understand what He's doing. I want to believe that the Lord is way smarter than I am. He gets it. His discipline is for my good.

Hebrews 12:7–8 tells the good but hard truth: **"It is for discipline that you have to endure. God is treating you as sons. For what son is there** whom his father does not discipline? If you are left without discipline, in which all have participated, then you are illegitimate children and not sons." Your Father loves you. Everything He allows is for your growth and good. He sees the long picture, even when you can't, and He lovingly draws near to you even in times of learning. (See Psalm 34:18.)

In the middle of my trial, God is present as a loving Father, disciplining His child.

_____

_____

_____

_____

_____

_____

_____

_____

_____

_____

_____

_____

_____

_____

_____

_____

_____

_____

_____

_____

_____

_____

_____

LESSON 12

God is never more present than when His children are suffering.
He is a faithful Friend, sustaining me.

1 Peter 4	James 1
Hebrews 12	2 Corinthians 12

GOD'S SUFFICIENT GRACE

I'm not much of an "original language" teacher. But once in a while in my study of a passage, I am rocked by some nuance of meaning I learn from the Bible's original language. I love the Greek word order of 2 Corinthians 12:9: **"Sufficient for you is the grace of Me."** That is an incredible promise! Sufficient for you is the grace of Me.

Think for a moment about the place where you meet with God. Your regular place. Is it a chair in your bedroom? Or at the kitchen table? Or as a father of five small children told me this week, is it the backseat of your car in the garage?

I can picture the place where I met with God years ago in my dorm room at college; I can picture where I met with God in the apartment where we lived in seminary; I can picture the little blue love seat that I used to sit on in our first house. I can picture my chair back at home right now where I meet with the Lord every day.

I find myself wondering, how many times have I gotten up from that place and left God's sufficient grace there? The Lord was there with me—holding out to me the grace for the trial I was going to face that day even as my mind was drifting off to my own plan. How many days did I run down the hall and off to my car and out to a busy day and leave Him sitting there with His sufficient grace?

If I'm going to live by that sufficient grace, I'm not going to catch it falling from the sky as I run to my next appointment. I've got to go to the fountain and drink deeply. He is the One who quenches my thirst—and yours. He is the One who fills up what's missing. He is the One who brings and sustains a continuous revival in your life.

He is that to every thirsty soul who comes to Him for life and breath. When a trial threatens to overwhelm you, remember God's promise: "Sufficient for today is the grace of Me." The Lord is a faithful friend, sustaining you.

_____

_____

_____

_____

_____

_____

_____

_____

_____

_____

_____

_____

_____

_____

_____

_____

_____

_____

_____

_____

_____

_____

_____

PRINCIPLE 4:

Until I embrace my trial in unwavering submission
to God, I will not reap the good.

Here's the final principle, again filled out by our four passages. *Until I embrace my trial in unwavering submission to God, I will not reap the good.* It really comes down to a choice. *Will I submit to God?*

Can I just tell you now that God wins? To resist God in any way is just to delay failure. Sooner or later, the flag will come down, the game will be over, and God will have won. Take a moment, figure out your chances of changing those odds, and get over onto God's side. Embrace your trial in unwavering submission to God.

"But I just don't see how I could ever embrace my trial," you say. "I don't think I'm able to." Okay, that's honest. But hear this: God made you; He knows what you're capable of and He never said you could do anything good in your own strength. You need Him to do it through you.

"Well, what is the good I will reap?" You can receive comfort and strength and wisdom and understanding. He will provide for your every need and fill your heart with a happiness that is incomparable in this world. You can win at things that matter if you submit to God. You can win in personal character. You can win in your family. You can win with your kids. You can win in your mind. You can win in your heart, in your soul. You can win for all eternity.

If you're against Him, you're gonna lose. And by lose I mean you're gonna get hurt. You're gonna suffer the consequences. You're gonna see your house crash. But if you submit to Him, you will reap the good.

Let these final four passages wash over you. Ponder these principles, one by one.

LESSON 13

Until I embrace my trial in unwavering submission to God, I will not reap the good.
The good doesn't come until I embrace my trial.

1 Peter 4	James 1
Hebrews 12	2 Corinthians 12

WHERE VICTORY BEGINS

If you're in a trial right now, your constant choice is whether you will embrace or resist what God is doing in your life.

Embracing God's purposes means you confess and live the reality that God is not asleep at the wheel. He is not AWOL. He's not running late for work. He's in control. He allowed this. You may wish it wasn't so, but He could have prevented this trial, and yet He didn't. You have to embrace that.

Resisting comes easier. We say, "No, not this." Or, "No, not now." Or, "No, not me." We storm into (or out of) God's presence with our demands. We fight against our pride, which blocks our view of God. And no matter how desperately we need God to show up in our lives, He doesn't as long as we resist His purposes.

I am aware of the weight of these words. I don't say them lightly, as though I could somehow just skip into that reality. I'm just telling you where the rock is so you can get your feet on it. If you're in the water right now and the waves are crashing, you've got to get back on solid ground. That's not going to happen until you embrace this trial.

Second Corinthians 12:10 says, **"For the sake of Christ, then, I am content with weaknesses."** The NIV says, "I delight in weaknesses." So many people don't get to this good place because they refuse to embrace the trial all the way to the end. They're like the farmer who never makes it to harvest time. Unless you embrace what God is doing with unwavering submission, you will not reap the good. Stay in the game. Don't resist.

Jesus Himself modeled this kind of victory in the garden when He prayed, **"Your will be done."** Not my will, God, but Your will. That's the essence of submission, and that's where the victory begins.

_____

_____

_____

_____

_____

_____

_____

_____

_____

_____

_____

_____

_____

_____

_____

_____

_____

_____

_____

_____

_____

_____

_____

_____

_____

LESSON 14

Until I embrace my trial in unwavering submission to God, I will not reap the good.

I can't embrace my trial without submitting to God.

| 1 Peter 4 | James 1 |
| Hebrews 12 | 2 Corinthians 12 |

FAILURE TO YIELD

Do you remember when we used to have those yellow triangle yield signs at intersections? Have you seen one lately? Unlikely. The traffic police had to make them all into four-way stops. Why? Because we stink at yielding. Each person drives up to the corner and thinks, *Clearly it's my right to go and the other driver needs to yield.* We had a lot of traffic crashes because no one wanted to yield.

More important than a crazy traffic sign, how good are you at yielding to God? Do you think, *Clearly, Lord, my way is better. This trial is taking my life in a direction that isn't in my plan so I'm going to run the sign.* Ever stop to think that this trial is God's way of saying, "I want to take your life in a different direction"?

Hebrews 12:9 says, **"Shall we not much more be subject to the Father of spirits and live?"**

The Greek word for "be subject to" is *hupŏtasō*, translated "submission" in other places in the New Testament. It's got a special twist in the original language, which means "submit yourself," as in, you're the one who willingly makes this choice.

God wants you to remain under the trial *by your own choice, willingly yielding yourself to God* so that **"the testing of your faith produces steadfastness"** (James 1:3). Remaining under the trial binds your heart to God. It will make you devoted and committed to Jesus Christ.

Submission doesn't come easily in a culture of individualism. We really like to think we can do things on our own, but the only way through this trial is to yield to God. You're headed for a wreck, until you let Him go first. *This isn't where I thought my life would be today, but I'm going to yield. I'm stopping, God. You go. I'm going to fall in behind You.* Let God have His way; yield to His purposes for your life. Embrace your trial by submitting to Him.

_____

_____

_____

_____

_____

_____

_____

_____

_____

_____

_____

_____

_____

_____

_____

_____

_____

_____

_____

_____

_____

_____

_____

LESSON 15

Until I embrace my trial in unwavering submission to God, I will not reap the good.

I can maintain my submission only through believing prayer.

1 Peter 4   James 1

Hebrews 12   2 Corinthians 12

MAKING IT STICK

How do you make it stick? How do you make your commitment to submit to God withstand the beating of the wind and waves of adversity? Great questions.

If you're like me, sometime in the past you've given something to God in full surrender only to wake up the next day with it back in your hands. *I gave this to God—what's it doing back here?*

On day one, I surrender to God that difficult something that threatens to take me under. *Here it is, God. Take it. Help me.* On day two—without even realizing it—I'm back in charge again. I'm nurturing my own set of rights and privileges. So back on my knees I go, submitting again to God. *Here I am again, God. My life is Yours. Not me, but You.*

So how do you stay there? I have found that the only way to maintain my submission to God is through believing prayer. Back on my knees, I give it back to God. I have to keep giving it back until I've broken the habit of taking it back.

James 1:6–8 says the doubting Christian is **"like a wave of the sea that is driven and tossed by the wind. For that person must not suppose that he will receive anything from the Lord; he is a double-minded man, unstable in all his ways."** The opposite of doubt is faith: standing on solid rock when the storm beats you from all sides. Believing prayer says, *Here I* *am again, God. I'm standing here on this rock. Here in this trial I'm standing still and strong.*

If you're in a trial right now, you need to be standing on that rock and praying like you've never prayed before. Surrender once again to God. Get up from your work, step aside from whatever you're doing, and give your burden to the Lord this moment, and day by day, and week by week. You can maintain your submission to God only through believing prayer. Embrace your trial by coming back to the throne of grace. There you are always welcome (see Hebrews 4:16).

LESSON 16

Until I embrace my trial in unwavering submission to God, I will not reap the good.

I will not reap the good unless I persevere.

1 Peter 4	James 1
Hebrews 12	2 Corinthians 12

YOU'RE NOT GOING UNDER

I've said it for years: There is nothing good that God brings into your life by way of transformation that He doesn't bring through the funnel of perseverance. If you let God place perseverance into your life, He can truly make you what He wants you to be.

First Peter 4:19 encourages us with, **"Let those who suffer according to God's will entrust their souls to a faithful Creator while doing good."**

Did you hear what you're supposed to do? Entrust your soul to your faithful Creator. God is faithful to you. He's got His hand on the thermostat. The fire will not get too hot. He's watching the depth gauge; this trial will not get too deep. God puts up the boundaries to your trials. *That's all. That's my daughter. I know what she can handle.* God protects His own. He will not allow you to be tried beyond what you are able to take. And in the middle of it all, He tells you to entrust yourself to His care.

God knows you better than you know yourself. You don't know what you are capable of when you're resting in God's strength and not your own. You're going to get through this one way or another. It's not going to last forever and you will get through it—*because God is faithful.*

Reassure yourself, *I'm not going under.* You can keep going for another day, another week because God is producing staying power in you. The ability to remain in that marriage—as hard as it is. The ability to remain in that job—as hard as it is. The ability to stick with it in that difficult circumstance—no matter what. If God can produce in you that staying power, He

can give you everything else. Listen, God can get every characteristic of
Christ into your life if He can just teach you to persevere.

_____

_____

_____

_____

_____

_____

_____

_____

_____

_____

_____

_____

_____

_____

_____

_____

_____

_____

_____

_____

_____

_____

_____

_____

_____

Your Prayer of Commitment

As we complete our time together, let me encourage you to pray a very specific prayer. Ask for His strength and grace to pray the following. Just tell Him:

Lord, I'm staying right here. I'm not looking for a way out. I'm remaining right here under the pressure.

And I yield. As best as I know how, God, I'm not fighting You. I'm not angry with You. I'm confused sometimes. I'm perplexed. I'm sad, but I'm not angry. I trust You.

I want to tell You, Lord, I'm not going to quit. By Your grace and in Your strength, I am not going to quit. I am going to keep doing the things You've called me to do. I'm going to keep believing the things I've always believed. I desire to get closer and deeper with You.

I am embracing this trial. I believe everything I've seen in this book about Your Word. I believe all of it. I'm treasuring these things in my heart and I'm committing to You once again here and now, God.

In Your sufficient grace I'm going forward. Turn these trials to gold in my life. I'm waiting to see it. My hope is in You. And I can wait.

In Jesus' name for His glory, amen.

FROM GOD'S HEART TO MINE

Romans 8:28

And we know that for those who love God all things work together for good, for those who are called according to his purpose.

Psalm 62:8

Trust in him at all times, O people; pour out your heart before him; God is a refuge for us.

MINING FOR GOLD

1. As we have done each time, pause and read again through the prayer of commitment at the end of the chapter. Hopefully it expresses the deepest desires of your heart, particularly as you continue to deal with ongoing trials.

2. As you review the short reflections on key Bible passages that make up this chapter, which one(s) have had particular impact on you? Why?

3. How would you summarize what you are taking away from this study?

4. Based on your study in this book and particularly what you know of God's Word, how would you demonstrate or illustrate each of the four principles of this book:

   • Every trial I face is allowed by God for my ultimate good.

   • Trials need not steal my joy.

   • God is never more present than when His children are suffering.

   • Until I embrace my trial in unwavering submission to God, I will not reap the good.

5. What people around you could you encourage with what you are taking away from this study?

6. Identify at least one way you can "boast" in the difficulties you are facing because you realize the way God is trying you is already producing gold.

EPILOGUE

THIS TRIAL COULD BE
THE BEST THING
THAT'S EVER HAPPENED
TO YOU

I hear a lot of people's stories about how they met God.

Several times in the past few years we have baptized more than three hundred adults in our church in a single weekend. Each person being baptized tells their story of how they came to Christ. When you listen to that many concurrent stories, you get a clear picture of how it happens. Their stories go something like this: "I was going along thinking I had it all together and then God dropped a boulder on my life. He got my attention! I had a problem and realized I couldn't handle it on my own so I reached out to the Lord; later I realized that it was really God reaching out to me."

While the label on the boulder may change and the individual uniqueness in each account is infinitely fascinating, the inner story that reveals God at work in someone's life does not vary. Bottom line: God uses the painful circumstances of life to soften human hearts and bring people to faith in Christ.

C. S. Lewis was right—pain *is* God's megaphone. He wouldn't use it if there was another way to get our undivided attention.

Is God getting your attention in this trial? Is this crisis bringing your need to the surface? Are your eyes opened to the fact that you need the Lord, not only for help in this trial, but because you're eternally lost? Now you realize He is standing right in front of you holding out His grace and all you need to do is reach out by faith and find Him.

God loves you. He loves you so much that He's allowed this trial to push you to the point where you have no choice but to look to Him. He loves you so much that He wants to give you eternal life in heaven. He doesn't expect you to earn it. He doesn't want you to beg or plead or try or work for it; He wants to give it to you. He requires nothing in return, except repentance and faith.

You receive eternal life by believing that God's Son died for your sin. You have to turn from your sin and trust, or believe, in Jesus as the only basis for your forgiveness. You must choose to believe.

God wants to save you; Jesus wants you to have the salvation He died to provide. You may be asking, saved from what? The answer is the penalty of your sin. If we refuse to embrace what God offers freely there remains no hope for your forgiveness. If you reject the only way to experience God's forgiveness, then you reject the only possibility of ever going to heaven.

Right now you could receive the gift of eternal life by getting on your knees all alone and praying a prayer something like this from your heart (also shown in chapter 1).

> *Dear Father in heaven,*
>
> *I know that I am a sinner and deserve eternal punishment. Thank You for loving me enough to send Your Son, Jesus into this world to die as payment for my sin. I repent of my sin and turn to You alone for my forgiveness. I believe that You are the only One who can cleanse my heart and change me. I now receive Jesus as the Savior and Lord of my life.*
>
> *Thank You for coming into my life and forgiving me of all my sin.*

Thank You for giving me the gift of eternal life! In the name of Jesus I pray, amen.

After praying this prayer, you may want to return to your heavenly Father to thank Him—yes, thank Him—for this crisis in your life that opened your eyes to your need and for holding out His saving grace.

If you've made a decision today to trust the Lord for your salvation and turn in repentance and faith to Him, please tell me about it. Write to letters@walkintheword.com. We would love to connect with you and help you in this important decision. I would also urge you to find a church in your area that will help you in this new life.

If you are already a Christian but hurting deeply, I urge you to remember the situation that prompted you to come to Christ in repentance and faith. Recall His grace in bringing you into the family.

Now, **"as you received Christ Jesus the Lord, so walk in Him"** (Colossians 2:6). Could this trial be a wake-up call to return to the Lord? Though you walk by faith and you love the Lord and Christ lives in you, there may be a body of sin that drags you down. If you've come to the place where you recognize that you've slipped away from the Lord, you need to have another crisis. You need the chords of commitment tightened up again that bind your heart to His.

Don't just cope with the difficult season as if it will eventually pass. Return to the Lord. Don't try to sneak back and pretend you never left—run hard back to Him in repentance and joy. He knows where you have been; where you are; and He wants your heart back with His.

God puts in front of us a lot of challenges that we want to attribute to circumstance—a difficult person, an area of conflict, a hardship that's dropped on our home or our marriage. In reality, that's God coming to you through that trial to advance your relationship with Him. Leave it up to us and we would hide or dodge these difficult things and not go anywhere good in our faith except in a steep, downward spiral.

I would exhort you as my brother or sister in the Lord to see every difficult circumstance that happens as God coming to you to advance His purposes for your life. Read this book through those eyes of faith. *What is it that you want to show me, Lord? I'm returning to You.*

Doubt can become faith. Discouragement can become joy. Despair can become purpose and fulfillment. Defeat can become victory. *How can that happen in your life?* I'm telling you how . . . come back to God.

NOTES

Chapter 2: Why Trials?

1. The story of Glen Chambers was told in a sermon by Chuck Swindoll. The accident is recorded at http://aviation-safety.net/database/record.php?id=19590623-1.

Chapter 3: What to Do with Trials

1. The letter is dated 29 May 2009 and is used by permission.

ACKNOWLEDGMENTS

Solomon was right when he noted, "Of making many books there is no end, and much study is a weariness of the flesh" (Ecclesiastes 12:12). Writing a book about the times when life is hard can itself become a hardship! I'm grateful I don't face any of life's difficulties alone. I'm in good company.

God continues to teach me the necessity of claiming, with Job, "But he knows the way that I take; when he has tried me, I shall come out as gold" (Job 23:10). God uses the writing of books, like everything else in life, as part of His refining process. I'm grateful to my Heavenly Father for His ever-wise working in my life to bring about His best.

When life is hard, the value of people who come alongside and help in practical ways becomes obvious and overwhelming. The folks I'm about to mention by name don't do their work in order to be acknowledged, which makes it all the more a pleasure to note their special roles. Each of them has been there during difficult times to make things easier. My thanks to:

- Ministry-through-publishing partners Moody Publishers, and in particular Greg Thornton and Jim Vincent, for their thorough editorial work and enthusiastic support of this project.
- Assistant-cum-laude Kathy Elliot, who graciously handles the myriad of daily details and keeps me from getting derailed by minutia in ministry.
- Writing partner Neil Wilson, who came alongside to help with the final "detailing" of the manuscript.
- The Walk in the Word staff under Janine Nelson's leadership of caring for all the teaching outlets for the message in this book.
- Barb Peil, who moved my messages from transcripts to a format that I could work on. Her efforts for the ministry of Walk in the Word have been tireless.
- Pastor Greg Laurie and Harvest Christian Fellowship of Riverside, California, who hosted Kathy and me during cancer treatments and provided a wonderfully supportive atmosphere for the original presentation of these messages.
- The members of Harvest Bible Chapel who have prayed us through these years and, more importantly, continue to faithfully pray and walk daily through both the hard and the easy times that God places before us.
- My wife, Kathy, and our children, Luke, Landon, and Abby, who have lived the day-by-day aspects of the various hard times mentioned in this book. Each of you is a special gift God has given me. One of the benefits of the hard times is that they highlight how precious you are to me. You, too, are on the way to coming out as gold.

Finally, my thanks to you who are reading this book in an effort to sense God's ways in your own life. May you, too, be able to say, with Job, "But he knows the way that I take; when he has tried me, I shall come out as gold" (Job 23:10).

LORD, CHANGE MY ATTITUDE

ISBN-13: 978-0-8024-3439-5

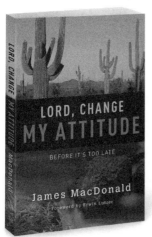

A bestseller since 2001, *Lord, Change My Attitude Before It's Too Late* is classic James MacDonald: bold, practical, and communicated in a way designed to set readers free from the negativity that erodes happiness. This new revision now includes study application questions in each chapter to help readers identify the attitudes of the heart that need change in order for God's abundance to flow. Pastor MacDonald shows readers how to begin to recognize wrong attitudes and work on replacing them with the right ones.

GRIPPED BY THE GREATNESS OF GOD

ISBN-13: 978-0-8024-4778-4

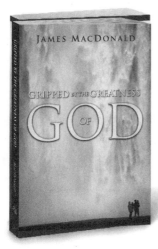

"God is not safe and He will not be squeezed into some neat, respectable Sunday discussion . . . No. To Know God at all is to watch Him explode any box we put Him in with His terror, majesty, and indescribable wonder."

Expounding on Isaiah's encounters with God, MacDonald prods snoozing saints to rediscover the wonder of God's attributes. *Gripped by the Greatness of God* will spur new and seasoned believers alike to detest mediocrity in their spiritual walks.

I REALLY WANT TO CHANGE
. . . SO HELP ME GOD

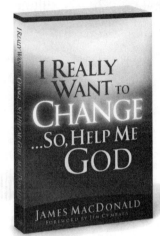

ISBN-13: 978-0-8024-3423-4

I REALLY want to change. Do you? Are you truly serious about allowing the power of God to transform your life? If you are, then prepare yourself for an incredible, life-changing experience. Change is difficult, but it's made even harder without practical guidance on how to do it. You will find that guidance in *I Really Want to Change . . . So, Help Me God*. James MacDonald is serious about the business of change according to God's Word. While many tell us that we should change and be more like Christ, MacDonald actually teaches us how to do it.

SEVEN WORDS TO CHANGE
YOUR FAMILY

ISBN-13: 978-0-8024-3440-1

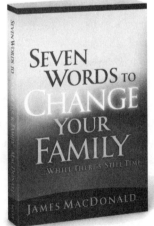

With the power of God your family can be totally transformed! For anyone who's serious about improving the quality of their family life, *Seven Words to Change Your Family* gives hard-hitting practical guidance on how to make it happen. In his captivating and contemporary style, Pastor James MacDonald will challenge readers to avoid devastating complacency and become proactive in loving their families. Whether it's learning to speak words of blessing, extend forgiveness, or be faithfully committed, families will be transformed by the step-by-step realistic plan laid out in this excellent resource.

WALK IN THE WORD

Walk in the **Word**
Dr. James MacDonald

Share the message
of *When Life Gets Hard*
with your church
or small group.

Look for LifeWay's *When Life Gets Hard*
Bible study in **Summer '10**.

Enjoy these other Bible studies
from James MacDonald:

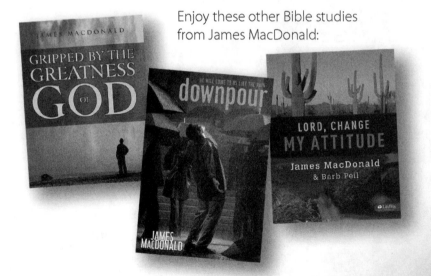